BEAUTY
FROM
ASHES

Walking in New Life with God after Loss

The journey of 9/11 widow Jean Braca

By Christmas M. Beeler

Table of Contents

"The Spirit of the Lord GOD is upon Me,
Because the LORD has anointed Me …
to heal the brokenhearted, to comfort all who mourn …
To give them beauty for ashes,
The oil of joy for mourning,
The garment of praise for the spirit of heaviness;
That they may be called trees of righteousness,
The planting of the LORD, that He may be glorified."
Isaiah 61:1-3

Jeanie would like to thank:
The Lord Jesus Christ
for being my Savior, my Husband, and my Best Friend.
My family for being there for me through this time,
and for the special bond that we share in the Lord.
Thanks to Christmas Beeler for being a blessing to work with.

Christmas would like to thank:
Jeanie, for her example as a Christian, a wife,
and a woman of God;
I look forward to seeing you again in our Father's house.
My husband David, a channel of Christ's love to me
in the tenderest of ways,
And my Savior Jesus Christ, the Author and Finisher.

HOW I MET JEANIE

God brings people into our lives to change us, to open our eyes to His eternal reality. Jeanie Braca has been one of those people for me, and I pray she will be for you. Wherever you are, whatever you are going through, Jeanie and I hoped this book would help you find comfort in our living, loving Savior, Jesus Christ.

As a writer for *Calvary Chapel Magazine*, I met Jean Braca through an article we did about God's work in New York after 9/11. Her husband Al had died in the Twin Towers leading people to Christ, and his story was told in several books and Christian articles worldwide. We did two follow-up stories on Jean and Al, and I felt God leading me to help tell her story. I visited her in New Jersey, interviewing many of her family members and friends. She showed me the program from the funeral, the melted credit cards that had been found in Al's wallet. Yet there was no heaviness, no anger in her countenance. She was full of the joy of the Lord. And I felt in my heart that the story we should tell was how she walked through her grief with the Lord—becoming not merely a 9/11 survivor but one who has drawn near to Him in affliction and has become a bright, beautiful light for Jesus Christ.

That is not to say she did not mourn. She loved Al deeply and was devastated by his loss. As you'll see in this book, she was genuine about the hard days, the step-by-step journey to find a new normal, a new life. And in surrendering to God and drawing near to Him, keeping a steady diet of reading God's Word and praising Him in her pain, she found her purpose. After Al's death, Jeanie helped spread the good news of God's forgiveness and salvation to thousands, sharing the stage with respected pastors like Mike Macintosh and Greg Laurie. She was invited to many events, conferences, schools, and churches to share with students, widows, and congregations. Instead of seeing 9/11 as a devastation that she had to somehow survive, she began to call it her "divine appointment"—something God had allowed for His purpose in her life.

Many days, her heart condition kept her confined to bed, but she continued to reach out to people with genuine love, comfort, and encouragement. She prayed for others daily. She wrote hundreds of letters and cards. She and I worked on this book for years. She told me how she wanted to live the rest of her life serving Jesus until she was taken home to be with her beloved husband.

We finished the final touches on this book in September of 2014. In October, she joined her husband in heaven. Despite publishing setbacks, I am pleased to bring to you the finished work. Jeanie hoped that it would help you draw closer to Jesus and find your healing and purpose in Him.

Christmas Beeler
January 2017

> ***You have turned for me my mourning into dancing;***
> ***You have put off my sackcloth and clothed me with gladness.***
> Psalm 30:11

AL'S LAST DAY

With his salt-and-pepper hair combed back neatly from his friendly, olive-skinned face, Al Braca paused at his work—perched high atop the New York skyline in the World Trade Center at Cantor Fitzgerald. He could see the heart of Manhattan from his desk; it was a sunny, clear morning with blue skies—September 11, 2001. He had paused from his work as a bond trader to savor a private thought of his wife Jeanie.

He hadn't kissed Jeanie goodbye that morning as was his usual custom. She looked so peaceful; he hadn't wanted to disturb her. Last night had been a special time of pouring their hearts out to each other—an emotional, tender time for both of them, a spontaneous celebration of their love after more than 30 years together.

So he had prayed over her silently in the quiet early morning hours, instead of out loud with his hand on her as he usually did, and then headed out the door. His family was his life, although he kept no photographs of them at his workplace.

His office and his home were two different worlds. He was always aware of the ungodliness around him and prayed constantly for himself and his coworkers. He had been the brunt of many jokes—derisively called "The Rev" because of his pure lifestyle. Once he had turned on his computer to find that someone had loaded it with pornographic images. Embarrassed, he had deleted them as his coworkers hooted with laughter. Another time, for his birthday, they had given him a cake with obscene decorations on it.

As a follower of Jesus Christ, Al was grieved by these things, but he tried hard to be an example without having a holier-than-thou demeanor. He didn't preach about his holy lifestyle, but made it clear that he would not go out drinking with them or to strip clubs. For one of his vacations, he had gone on a Christian men's retreat—to the shock of his coworkers, most of whom worked hard and played harder on the weekends. He never tried to hide that he was deeply committed to his wife, his family, and his Lord.

He didn't despise his coworkers; rather, their lifestyles broke his heart. He and Jeanie had spent hours praying for his colleagues. He couldn't help but pray—hearing about their marriages in trouble, their affairs, the burdens of their souls, their addictions. Many were the times someone would approach him in private to ask for counsel or prayer for a struggling marriage or a seriously ill family member. Al would always listen with compassion and pray; often he would share how Jesus Christ had changed his life. Over and over, he told men that the riches and power and women of this life would never satisfy them. He shared that Jesus Christ died to set them free from sin and give them a truly abundant life following Himself—an eternal life.

Suddenly, a terrible boom vibrated through the building.

People jumped out of their seats and ran to the windows. Flames and smoke billowed up from somewhere below. Most of them had been there in 1993, when a truck bomb below the North Tower had caused quite a scare—evacuating both of the Twin Towers, killing six people, and injuring thousands more. But things had been relatively peaceful for the last eight years.

Nervous voices tried to stay calm as people asked, "What's going on?"

"What was that—a bomb?"

Al did not panic, but he began to pray. They waited for news, an announcement of some kind—but no word came. The flames were getting bigger, the smoke thicker. People started to comment that the air was getting warm in the office. A growing fear began rising in Al's mind that something was terribly wrong. Suddenly, another awful boom sounded—this time farther away—and they all saw with horror that the second tower was on fire. Voices began to rise; people were starting to panic.

Looking around the room, Al felt the Holy Spirit speak to his heart. He knew clearly that God was calling him to minister to his coworkers in the midst of this strange battle. He realized that they all might die, and if so, this would be his last chance to share the Gospel with them. Maybe now, with death staring them in the face, they would listen. Maybe now—when money could not help them, when there was nowhere else to go—they would turn to God. With a quiet urgency and supernatural confidence, Al walked to the middle of the room and climbed on top of a desk.

His coworkers looked up at him in surprise. Some of them were crying; some of them were pale with fear. Some had been pacing near the windows, waiting for a rescue. Everyone stopped and looked up at Al.

Taking a deep breath and praying a silent prayer, Al said loudly and clearly, "I'm going to heaven—who's coming with me?"

Several gathered around the table, looking up at him. He could see they were listening now. There were no jeers, no smirks. All eyes were fixed hungrily on him. As Al spoke, one of the men called his home to leave a message that Al was leading them in prayer. Another person sent a similar message to a loved one through email as the Towers burned.

With love and urgency, Al shared that even though every person has sinned, Jesus Christ paid for the sins of all by dying on the cross in their place. If they would accept Christ as their Lord and Savior now, repent of their sins, and entrust their souls fully to Him, He would forgive their sins and grant them entrance to heaven. All they had to do was believe, truly believe, and turn to Christ. "Pray with me," Al said. Heads around him bowed; some prayed aloud, some silently. He urged them to trust in Jesus.

The room was getting hotter, filling with smoke. People were coughing; everyone was sweating. Al realized that he was going to see his Savior that day. His heart broke as he thought of his beloved Jeanie and their children. He picked up a phone and tried several times until he got a dial tone. He tried to call the house but couldn't get through:

the lines were all jammed. Praying for help, he dialed "0" and got an MCI operator.

His voice husky from breathing in smoke, he said, "You've got to help me. My name is Al Braca. I'm in the World Trade Center, and I need you to get a message to my wife and family." The lady operator sounded alarmed but agreed to take his message; her name was Wilma.

Urgently, Al said, "I feel like my feet are on fire. I'm not going to make it. Will you tell my family that I love them? Tell my wife Jeanie and my children that I love them. Tell them not to worry about me."

He could hear Wilma crying. "Promise me that you'll tell my wife Jeanie." She agreed to tell his family. Coughing from the smoke, Al gave her Jeanie's name and home phone number and had her repeat it back to him. They had to get this message. He wanted them to know that he loved them, that they were on his mind in his last moments, and that he knew he was going home to be with the Lord. She promised again to relay his message. They talked for a few seconds more, and then the line went dead. He slowly hung up the phone. *I'm coming home, Lord,* he prayed. Smoke filled the room, his lungs; he passed out. A few hours later, the Twin Towers collapsed.

Meditation:

Precious in the sight of the LORD
Is the death of His saints.
Psalm 116:15

As you think about your loved one's last moments, remember that God our Father was there in their final moments. Thank Him now for being present with them.

We are confident, yes, well pleased rather to be absent from the body
and to be present with the Lord.
2 Corinthians 5:8

If your loved one was a believer, you can be confident that—although they are absent from your presence—they are now in the presence of the Lord. Ask the Lord to help you find peace in knowing that they are not gone; they are simply Home.

For "whoever calls on the name of the LORD shall be saved."
Romans 10:13

Al knew he was going to heaven because he had accepted Christ as his Savior. If you don't know for certain that you would go to heaven when you die, stop now and pray to the Lord sincerely from your heart. Confess that you are a sinner; ask Him to forgive your sins; thank Him for forgiving you because of the sacrifice Christ made on the cross. Find a church that teaches the Bible—such as a Calvary Chapel—to help you to grow in your faith.

Chapter 1

DADDY'S NOT COMING HOME

God is our refuge and strength, a very present help in trouble.
Psalm 46:1, NKJV

That beautiful September morning, Jeanie Braca sat in her favorite white armchair near her bedroom window, reading her Bible and praying. She felt so peaceful. Her thoughts drifted to the night before, when her husband Al had held her in his arms and whispered sweet words that had deeply touched her heart. She savored her memory of their conversation as they had lain in bed together. Even though they had been married for 33 years, they had said things to each other last night that they never had before.

"I've learned so much from you, Jeanie," Al had said. His words surprised Jeanie, who had always felt that Al was in some ways superior to her since he came from a wealthier, more refined family. As they held one another close, they talked about how much they loved each other. They both already had a deep security in the other's love, but that night they put it into words—sweet, tender words. "I am so thankful God gave you to me," he had said. He praised her for being a godly wife and mother, for taking care of their home, and for being a great support and help to him. As his words of praise, love and appreciation filled her ears, her heart was filled with a sense of well-being and thankfulness to God. *Finally, I have become the wife I have prayed to be,* she thought. Many times she had read about the virtuous wife in Proverbs 31 and asked God to teach her how to be a godly wife and mother—to speak with kindness, to be hard-working, to take care of her husband, her children, and their home.

In turn, Jeanie had told Al how grateful she was to have a husband who loved the Lord, who loved her, and loved their children. They rejoiced together, recounting how they both had given their hearts and lives to Jesus when their children were young—nearly 23 years ago. God had changed their lives and then used them to encourage other couples. "We're going to have a wonderful life together," Al had said. She could tell from his voice that he was smiling. They talked happily about their retirement plans, when Al would leave his high-pressure job as a vice president and bond broker for Cantor Fitzgerald and open a pizzeria. He and their son-in-law Greg wanted to use the pizzeria to welcome teens for Bible studies. With three of their four children grown and moved out, Al and Jeanie had just sold their large home, moved into a smaller house in Leonardo, NJ, and were planning a trip to Hawaii. Their present life together was so sweet, and the future looked even more promising.

Jeanie nestled deeper into in her armchair with appreciation. Even this pristine, white chair was a representation of new beginnings. She had gotten it after recovering from prolonged health problems which had prohibited her from owning white furniture. For years she had problems with feminine hemorrhaging and heavy bleeding. But, after undergoing surgery, she had been healed—which she credited to God—and now could enjoy having white furniture for the first time in years. So her chair was more than just a chair to her: It was a celebration, a sign of healing and new beginnings and good things ahead. Her prolonged heart condition was also finally under control. She sighed in contentment.

Feeling optimistic and peaceful, she closed her Bible and prayed aloud, "What would You like to talk about this morning, Lord?" Jeanie shared a close personal relationship with her Savior, Jesus Christ. She knew He listened to her prayers, as He promised in His Word, and often she could feel Him speak quietly to her heart. As she talked to her Savior, suddenly she felt an impression that her husband would go home to heaven that day. She was shocked and immediately put the thought out of her mind, thinking that the enemy was trying to cause her fear. It was the morning of September 11, 2001, and she knew that her husband Al, 54, was working on the 104th floor of the World Trade Center in Tower One.

She stepped outside to mail some bills. *What a beautiful sunny day,* she thought. Coming inside, she flipped on the TV. It was a few minutes until 9 a.m.; maybe the weather report would come on. The screen was still fuzzy because their cable wasn't hooked up yet; they hadn't been in their new home a month. Suddenly, Jeanie was motionless, blinking and staring at the screen. One of the Twin Towers was on fire—it was Al's building.

Her first reaction was concern, but she wasn't afraid. Assuming that the NY Fire Department would be able to extinguish the fire, Jeanie's biggest concern was for her mother in law, who was recovering from breast cancer surgery. She dialed her number and reassured her, "He's going to be okay; don't worry about it." However, while she was on the phone, Jeanie saw the second tower being hit. She quickly ended the call and waited to learn more. Soon, her phone was ringing off the hook.

She recalled February of 1993, when a car bomb had been detonated in the basement of Al's building in an attempt to destroy it and the other tower. Though six people had died, everyone else in the Twin Towers had evacuated and survived. Al had ministered to his coworkers and other evacuees. He helped a frightened woman, who had difficulty walking because of health problems, make her way down the multiple flights of steps. He had come home late that night, sharing stories of how God had used him to pray for people and share the Gospel. She was sure this day would end the same way.

Soon, her house was full of friends and family—her grown children and their families—encouraging her, praying, and offering their support. She sensed that many people were being cautious about what they said; perhaps they were waiting for her to start panicking. But she wasn't afraid; she believed Al would come home. But as the day wore on, a nagging feeling rose in the back of her mind that something wasn't right. He hadn't called. She reassured herself that Al was probably just busy ministering to people like he had during the bombing eight years ago.

Jeanie went through the day in a daze. No one would let her return upstairs to look at the television; she knew they were worried about her heart condition. She had suffered congestive heart failure in February of 2000. One of her sons called Jeanie's doctor to prescribe some pills in case the shock sent her heart into relapse. But Jeanie was calm, checking her watch, waiting for Al to come home.

Finally, after 6 pm, Jeanie was sitting outside on the deck with a handful of close friends and family. She commented, "I wonder when Daddy's coming home? You'd think he would have called by now." Her oldest son David sat down on the steps next to Jeanie, took her hands in his, and looked steadily into her eyes. He said, "Mom, there's no longer a World Trade Center. Both towers have collapsed. We're under attack, even at the Pentagon. Daddy isn't coming home."

Jeanie blinked in amazement. "Are you sure?" He nodded. She tried hard to digest his words. Then, as if of their own accord, tears began falling and words started tumbling forth: "But we have plans: He's retiring, we're going to Hawaii." Her mind raced, trying to comprehend what had happened, and she forced herself to picture the towers collapsing. In that horrible moment, she realized that no one could have survived. Al was gone.

Her voice rose in agony as she said, "My life is in that building. And it's come down, and there's nothing left." She crumpled to her knees, praying, "God, help me. Please show me the way I need to go. I'm not going to make it without You."

Her friends and children gathered around her, hugging her and praying for her. She felt their hands on her shoulders, felt their arms around her. Jeanie and her children—David and Christine, Christina and Greg, Deanna and Shawn, and Christopher—wept together. Finally, Jeanie rose heavily to her feet and said, "Please, I need to be alone with my Savior." She went inside, past the others who were gathered downstairs, and quietly went up to her room.

She looked again at the white chair, this time remembering that it was the first piece of furniture Al had bought for their new home. Just this morning, life had seemed full of possibilities. Now she could see nothing ahead but emptiness. This was where she had started her day with the Lord. Well, here she would end her day—also with the Lord.

Sitting down in the chair, she whispered through tears, "Father, if there's one thing I could ask of You: Could You please get all of the honor and glory in this terrible moment in my life? Please, make sure I stay close to You because I don't know if I can do this." Her voice

15

broke; she paused and continued. "I want to, with all my heart. I want You to be proud of me." She thought about her greatest desire for the past 23 years, of standing before the throne of God where she hoped to hear Him say something like: "Jeanie Barone Braca, well done. You did everything I called you to do."

As the darkness of evening gathered outside her window, Jeanie sat alone in her chair trembling. She knew that her life—as she had known it—was over. Again she forced her shocked mind to accept the fact that the towers had collapsed; she faced the awful truth that Al was never coming home. How was she going to make it without him? "God, please show me the way. Show me that You love me, that You still care, that You're here." The sense of His presence filled her heart and mind. From that moment on—through the dark and painful days, in valleys and in moments of peace, through times of solitude and times of fellowship—she felt His hedge of protection around her.

Meditation

God is our refuge and strength, a very present help in trouble.
Therefore we will not fear,
Even though the earth be removed,
And though the mountains be carried into the midst of the sea;
Psalm 46:1-2

Whatever you are going through today—whatever emotions or circumstances—know that God is with you. When the earth shakes, He is your refuge—your strong tower, your hiding place. His presence is your safe place. He is your strength; He does not expect you to be strong in your own power. He holds us up when we are weak.

When the mountains in our life crumble—when a loved one departs this earth—we go through so many emotions: shock, grief, even fear. We may wonder how we will find the strength to go on. But we can hide in the Lord's faithful presence; He will never leave us. He is right here with you today.

Chapter 2

BOY MEETS GIRL

Therefore we will not fear, even though the earth be removed, and though the mountains be carried into the midst of the sea.
Psalm 46:2

Jeanie woke up alone in their bed the next morning, instantly gripped by the startling reality that Al was gone. Just yesterday she had glimpsed him dash out the door on his way to work. He hadn't kissed her goodbye that morning like he normally did, probably because he wanted to let her sleep. This morning she lay still in the quiet room, her thoughts drifting to Al.

She remembered the first time she had seen him: They were just children. Growing up in an Italian neighborhood on Staten Island, NY, she was at her uncle's apartment in the New Brighton area when she had seen a little dark-haired boy come to the door with his father to collect the rent. She found out later that the boy was Al Braca.

Twelve years later, when she was a teenager, Jeanie would call her friend Diane at her grandmother's house every Sunday afternoon to say hello. Italian families in their neighborhoods often got together for meatballs and macaroni on Sundays. Diane had a cousin named Al, and he would also talk to Jeanie on the phone. Though they never met, their conversations would often last a while. He would make her laugh, telling stories about his family and his various girlfriends. Jeanie, normally shy around strangers, felt at ease talking to Al. Though they had never met in person, they talked on the phone almost every Sunday afternoon for a year until Al went off to study business at college.

When he came back for Christmas vacation, Al called Jeanie to ask her to a New Year's Eve party. Jeanie declined, as her previous boyfriend had just left for Vietnam, and she wasn't ready to date someone else. She didn't mention that she had heard about Al's dating habits—especially that he was cheap on dates. Jeanie didn't think he was her type.

A year later, Jeanie finally met him face to face on the Staten Island Ferry. On a brisk January day in 1967, Jeanie was on the ferry with two other girlfriends when she ran into her friend Marty in the ladies' room. Marty told her, "I'm here with Freddie." Jeanie realized this was her chance to meet the young man she had spoken to for a year.

Stepping out onto the deck, Jeanie's eyes searched the passengers and spotted a young man sitting beside Marty: Al was tall and thin with glasses. Her first impression was that he had a very smart, collegiate appearance. His black hair had early flecks of gray; he wore a sports jacket and a tie. She knew he was already working as a clerk on Wall Street at age 20. Jeanie was 19, also with glasses, twinkling blue eyes, and shoulder-length auburn hair. Though Marty introduced Al as "Freddy," one of his nicknames, Jeanie decided to address him instead as Al, the name she had used when they spoke on the phone together. "Hi, Al, I'm Jeanie." He looked at her blankly.

"Don't you know who I am?" Jeanie asked. He shook his head no.

She explained, "I'm Jeanie Barone, the girl you talk with on the phone every Sunday."

His blank expression turned to a wide grin. He jumped up, hugged her, and kissed her on the cheek, saying, "Jeanie! I have wanted to meet you!" After talking with Al and Marty for a few minutes, Jeanie and her girlfriends went their way. Across the ferry boat, Jeanie caught Al looking her direction. He winked at her, and she turned her head away, feeling uncomfortable that he would flirt with her while he was with another girl. The next day, Al called Jeanie. During their conversation, she suggested he go out with her other friend, Patty, and he did.

A short time later, Al and Patty had broken up, and Jeanie saw him again on the ferry. As they talked, Al casually said, "So, Jeanie, when are you going to ask me out?"

Jeanie coldly replied, "I always thought a gentleman asked a lady out." Then she walked away. Though it was 1967 and many girls were initiating relationships with guys, Jeanie was not. Any man that wanted to win her heart was going to have to work for it. He had to be sincere; she wasn't into playing games.

He followed her, polite and charming—chatting with her and making her laugh. Then he asked her again: "So, when do you want to go out?"

Miffed by his seemingly nonchalant attitude about dating her, Jeanie said, "Never. Are you crazy? I know all your secrets, how you are with girls. You dated two of my friends. I will not go out with you!" Not only was Al known to be cheap on his dates, but Jeanie suspected that he was a mama's boy—used to getting his own way.

To her surprise, he said, "I've got news for you, Jeanie Barone: I'm going to ask you until you go out with me, and you're going to go out with me, and we're going to go steady, get engaged, and then get married." Jeanie rolled her eyes at him, though inside she couldn't help thinking that he was funny. He walked her to the bus stop, saying he would call her that night, and recited her phone number. Jeanie was impressed that he had it memorized. Maybe she wasn't just another pretty face to him after all. When she got home, Jeanie found her mother on the phone, laughing and talking.

Her mother called out: "Oh Jeanie, that nice boy Al is on the phone." Jeanie's face turned red with anger. So this was his strategy—Al was going to butter up her mother!

Holding her hand over the receiver, Jeanie said, "Mom! What are you doing? Don't get involved."

Her mother urged, "But he sounds like a really nice guy, Jeanie. You should go out with him." Jeanie talked briefly with Al and held her ground that she would not go out with him.

A few months later, one of Jeanie's cousins died unexpectedly. She was too upset to go to the viewing—especially because it was the Saturday before Easter. While she stayed home alone, Al called her. She talked about her cousin; Al listened. Their conversation was easy, like it was the year before when she had talked to him every weekend. They talked all day—from 11 that morning to 11 o'clock that night. She had never found someone so easy to talk to. He made her feel special, listening respectfully to her thoughts and feelings. They laughed together; he allowed her to cry. She realized that there was more to Al Braca than she thought.

He asked her out again, and she agreed to go to a concert with him on April 1, 1967. He pointed to a pair of empty seats. As they were making their way over, they spotted some friends heading toward the same seats. Al's face went white; Jeanie knew instantly that he hadn't bought tickets—he was going to *steal* their seats! Furious, she demanded, "Did you pay for our seats?" He shrugged it off with a laugh. "Al, if you don't go pay for tickets, I'm walking home." Flashing her a mischievous smile, Al good-naturedly went back and bought tickets.

Soon Al began telling their friends and some of her cousins that he and Jeanie were getting married. When Jeanie heard second-hand his presumptions, she was livid. This spoiled young man wasn't going to get her hand in marriage so easily. He hadn't even asked her! If he really loved her, he would have to show her.

So the next time she saw him, she walked past him, casually throwing over her shoulder, "Oh, hi Al." She knew it drove him crazy. Repeatedly, she ignored him until eventually Al realized that Jeanie wanted to be treated like a lady. He began taking her to nice restaurants and romantic places; they dated for more than a year. They laughed a lot together and grew steadily closer. They spent hours talking about their dreams, their childhoods, and their hopes for the future. As they talked about their Italian families, they realized that Al's family had owned her uncle's building. When the Bracas learned that Al was dating a girl whose family had little money, they opposed the match. Nonetheless, Jeanie and Al picked out wedding rings, each making a small payment every week until the other's ring was paid off. They got married in a traditional church in Stapleton on October 13, 1968.

Alone in their room that morning, Jeanie smiled as she remembered the cocky young man she had first met on the ferry so long ago.

Turning her thoughts to the Lord, Jeanie asked for strength to face the day—her first day in 33 years without her beloved Al. She knew that awaiting her was a mountain of decisions about the memorial service and adjusting to a new life without the man who had become her best friend on earth.

She would need God's strength. As she looked around their bedroom, her eye fell on Al's Bible. Pulling it from the shelf, she began tenderly flipping through the pages. This was the Bible he had read every morning to prepare himself for the day. Sometimes he would write down things that God had shown him through the Word; sometimes he would share those things with Jeanie and their family. As she turned the pages, Jeanie noticed a piece of paper with Al's handwriting. Unfolding it, she held her breath as she read what appeared to be a letter from the Lord to Al that he had written down. It read:

> *"The more you trust Me, the more I will bless you. The more faith you have in Me, the more I will work in you. The more you seek Me, the more I will teach you and show you the miracles I can do.*
>
> *Do not fear for your life because I control your destiny, not the world. If you belong to Me, then who has control of you and your future? No one else but Me. Trust in Me, have faith in Me, and I will wipe out all your fears and anxieties. No one can touch you or harm you. If I am in you and you in Me, then you have My power over all your problems.*
>
> *So seek Me, trust Me, and have faith in Me; these are the keys to your success. I love you and want no harm to come to you and your family."*

Jeanie's eyes filled with tears. She had never seen this letter before; it must have been something that the Lord had spoken to Al recently. But as she considered the words, she didn't understand. The letter said that God did not want harm to come to Al or his family—yet Al was dead. Pain pierced her heart. Finally, her voice thick with emotion, she prayed, "I don't understand, Lord. I don't understand." She sat in her chair for quite a while, clutching the letter in her hands. Finally, she surrendered her heart to the Lord. Even though she still didn't fully understand, she decided to trust Him.

"Oh Father," she said softly, "Did You remind him of this letter yesterday when the building was burning? Did You remind Him that you will take care of us?"

Her eyes lovingly traced the lines of her husband's handwriting. Some might argue that harm *had* come to her family in losing Al, but Jeanie realized that God had made her husband a promise—that He would look after their family. She read again that God, not the world, controlled Al's destiny. He had allowed Al to be taken at this time, in this way. And she knew that—because he had trusted Christ as his Savior—Al was in heaven with the Lord. Everything was still in God's hands. She knew the Holy Spirit was giving her clarity and comfort. "Thank You, Father. Thank You for this," she prayed, clutching the letter. She folded it carefully and put it back in the Bible, where she would revisit it many times to be reminded and encouraged by the promises God had made to her husband before his death.

Meditation

Your eyes saw my substance, being yet unformed.
And in Your book they all were written,
The days fashioned for me,
When as yet there were none of them.
Psalm 139:16

Before you were born, God knew you. He knew your loved one. He has watched over you every day of your life. He has been with you through all of the happy moments with your loved one. He fashioned those days for you and for them. Now that they are gone, He is still with you. He knows you. Though it may feel like your life has ended, He has more days ahead for you.

Chapter 3

JEANIE'S TESTIMONY

The Lord has done great things for us, and we are filled with joy.
Psalm 126:3, NIV

As she prayed and drew near to God, Jeanie remembered when the Lord had first become real in her own life. In fact, she remembered the exact moment.

It was March of 1977; she and Al had been married for almost 10 years. She was sitting alone in a relative's Staten Island home with tears streaming down her face, an open Bible on her lap. Doctors had just called to tell her that her 4 ½-year-old daughter would probably not live much longer.

Two days before, Christina became very sick and was put into the hospital. At that point, all the doctors had known was that the girl's blood counts were spiraling despite multiple transfusions. Her blood count needed to be 12, but it had dwindled to 3. They tried several treatments and transfusions, but her count went down to 2. Jeanie, herself unwell, had gone to change at the nearby home of Al's Aunt Anna and Uncle Jack. The doctor, Uncle Louie, called and told Al, "You had better pray, because there's nothing else we can do. At any moment, God could take her." Christina's condition was critical: Her kidney, liver, and heart were enlarged. Doctors gave the child 72 hours to live.

Jeanie was shaken; she needed God's help like never before. She remembered what her sisters Sue and Mary Ann had recently told her—that God wanted to have a personal relationship with her and that He spoke through His word.

Her sisters Sue and Mary Ann left the Catholic church years ago and recently had started attending an evangelical church. In a spirit of love and excitement over their new faith, they had been sharing the Gospel with Jeanie for the past several months. Mary Ann said that even though she had believed in Christ before, she hadn't known Him as her personal Savior until now. She explained that neither good works nor church membership would pay for sins; only the blood of Christ Himself could cleanse a person and give eternal life. She shared what Jesus said to Nicodemus in John 3, that a person *"must be born again."*

At first, Jeanie had been furious with them. She had always considered them the wild and rebellious members of the family, leaving the Catholic church. Who were they to tell her that she wouldn't go to heaven? Or to lecture her on being right with God? How could they say that they had the answer and Jeanie did not? She considered herself a faithful church member and a good person.

Jeanie had been skeptical of their new faith, but today she was desperate. Both Mary Ann and Sue encouraged Jeanie to read her Bible. Maybe they were right. Maybe God did speak to people—personally, right from His Word.

In a desperate attempt to hear from God, Jeanie sat down at the table with Uncle Jack's Bible. Not knowing what to read, she let the book fall open, placed her finger on the page, and peered through tears at the words:

But when Jesus heard it, He answered him, saying, "Do not be afraid; only believe, and she will be made well." Luke 8:50

She was stunned: could these words be for her? She read the entire story of Jairus' little daughter who had gotten so sick and died, yet Jesus had raised her from the dead. Then she stared again at His words in verse 50: *"Only believe, and she will be made well."* Jeanie's heart was racing; she felt that God was right there with her. She could feel Him speaking to her through the words. In response, her tears of sorrow turned to tears of passionate faith, and she cried out, "Yes, Lord, I believe!" As Jeanie clung to her newfound faith in God's promise, Christina lived through the night. And another.

A few days later, little Christina told her mother that she'd had a visitor—a man wearing a long robe and sandals. He told her that, no matter what the doctors said, God was going to heal her. And she was to "tell mommy" what the man had said. Jeanie held that promise in her heart. She would believe God no matter what happened.

After that day at Uncle Jack's house, everything was different. Over the next few months, as Christina's condition remained tenuous, Jeanie's faith grew stronger. Their family doctor wrote an article in a medical journal; a team of doctors from all over the country got involved. They concluded that the little girl had a rare blood disease called hemolytic anemia and asked to study her as a test case. They warned Jeanie that Christina would probably never recover and not to expect the impossible. Yet Jeanie clung to her faith in God's promise. She continued to pray for her little girl and read the Bible.

Al had a difficult time. As Christina's illness dragged on and on with little improvement, it began to wear down his optimistic outlook. One day, as Al and Jeanie were driving to the hospital, he started crying. Jeanie urged him to pull over. He began to sob. "I'm so angry; how could God do this to us? Why would he take away our baby?" Jeanie hugged him and reassured him that somehow God would heal Christina. Broken with sorrow, Al started shouting through his tears at God, "Why are You doing this to my little girl?"

Though still attending the Catholic church with Al, Jeanie also began going to a Pentecostal Christian church with her sisters. She realized that she had to trust in Christ and His work on the cross to save her—nothing else.

She read Ephesians 2:8-9, which say, *"For by grace you have been saved through faith, and that not of yourselves; it is the gift of God, not of works, lest anyone should boast."*

Jeanie realized that she had been trusting in her own goodness to save her. If God had told her before that she wasn't forgiven, she probably would have argued with Him. She imagined herself saying proudly, "But I've done this and this. I've gone to church all of my life."

Christina's illness was the catalyst that changed Jeanie's life. She met Christ personally that year—at age 30. She accepted Christ as her personal Savior and chose to follow Him once and for all. She knew that it was by His blood, by His sacrifice alone, that she was forgiven. She opened her heart to Him and was reborn by His Holy Spirit. She took all of her children to church to learn about Jesus.

Jeanie had told Al about the promise in Luke 8 and what the Lord had spoken to her. He had listened but continued to go to the Catholic church. Jeanie knew that Al saw a change in her: She listened to Christian music at home, read her Bible, and talked openly about what God was teaching her. But she never argued with him about church; instead, she showed him love and respect and prayed for him. As a gift to Jeanie for Mother's Day, the children asked Al to come to church with them. So on Mother's Day, 1978, Al came to the evangelical church for the first time.

For the next few weeks, Al continued to attend church and read the Bible. Finally, one Sunday morning after hearing the Gospel message, Al leaned over to Jeanie and whispered, "I'm ready." When the pastor gave the invitation, Al went forward to accept Christ. Soon after, they moved to Middletown, NJ, and began attending Calvary Chapel Four Winds. As they grew in their faith together, they continued to cling to God's promise about Christina.

For five years, Christina's health constantly fluctuated—she would improve, then decline again. Doctors had told Jeanie several times that she needed to accept that Christina might not make it, but she would tell them, "The Lord is going to heal her." Christina herself had come to believe in Christ and in God's promise about her healing. One day, after another exhausting series of needles and tests at the hospital, the 10-year-old girl turned to Jeanie and said, "Mommy, I really want to trust Jesus for the rest of my life."

"You know, Christina, so do I!" Jeanie had replied.

They went back to their family doctor—affectionately nicknamed "Uncle Louie"—and told him that they were through with tests and treatments. They were going to totally entrust Christina into the Lord's hands, and they believed God would make her fully well.

That year, Christina's condition was completely healed and never returned. Jeanie and Al knew that God had answered their prayers and fulfilled the promise He had made five years before to Jeanie through the story of Jairus' daughter in the Gospel of Luke. The entire Braca family came to accept Christ—because of the miracle of Christina's healing and because of seeing the changes in both Al and Jeanie. The Bracas were a witness to everyone who came into their home, testifying about the miracle God had done for them and sharing the Gospel. They couldn't stop talking about Christina's healing.

Jeanie and Al began ministering to couples—a ministry they would do together for 25 years both at their Pentecostal church in Staten Island and later at CC Four Winds in Middletown, NJ. When couples would share about the struggles they were going through, Al would tell them about Christina: "God did the impossible for us; He healed our daughter." He would then read the story of Jairus's daughter in Luke 8 with them, encouraging them that nothing is impossible for the Lord; He can heal any illness and help in any situation.

While working on Wall Street, Al would often open a conversation by saying, "Can I tell you about a miracle God did in my life?" Then he would share Christina's story. His angry tears had turned to joy, and he wanted to share their beautiful miracle with as many people as he could.

Alone in her bedroom, Jeanie smiled as she remembered Al's zeal for sharing about Christina's healing. His eyes would shine, and he would practically glow. Al had touched so many people. They had seen dozens of couples grow closer to the Lord and to each other. Al had lived his life to the fullest for Christ. Her eyes welled with tears, but this time, they were tears of joy. She thanked God for saving their family and giving her such a godly husband. They had enjoyed many rich, wonderful years together. And because they had both entrusted their lives to Jesus, she knew they would spend eternity together.

Though she missed him terribly, she knew that Al was waiting for her in heaven with their Savior.

Meditation

The Lord has done great things for us,
and we are filled with joy.
Psalm 126:3, NIV

As you look back on your life with your loved one, think of the joyful times you had together. Treasure those times. Think of the miracles that God did in your lives; remember how He used that person to touch your life and the lives of other people.

To everything there is a season
… a time to weep, and a time to laugh
Ecclesiastes 3:1a, 4a

Though you may still be mourning, there may come moments of laughter as well. It is all right to laugh. It is good to rejoice in what God did in your lives together. It is also all right to weep. The Lord laughs with you, and He weeps with you.

Chapter 4

AMELIA'S VISION

"The hair of their head was not singed nor were their garments affected,
and the smell of fire was not on them."
Daniel 3:27b

A few days after September 11, Jeanie went downstairs and looked around her empty house. It had been full of friends and family since the attacks, but now it was quiet. Christopher was at school. She surveyed the disheveled rooms and knew it was time to call Amelia. Amelia Okpanachi was Jeanie's housekeeper. After Jeanie had suffered heart failure, Al had initially taken care of Jeanie himself but eventually needed to return to work. He hired Amelia, who also worked for their friends Gary and Peggy Cuozzo. Over the past few months, Jeanie had become friends with the honest-talking, hard-working African pastor's wife who was a strong, born-again Christian.

Amelia let herself in and found Jeanie in the kitchen, seated at the table. Jeanie had started tidying before Amelia got there, but found that her energy ran out quickly. Having Amelia's familiar presence was comforting to Jeanie, who felt as if her life had been turned upside down. She was still trying to comprehend what had happened, still trying to find her footing. They hugged in greeting, as they always did, but this time they held each other tightly. Both women's eyes welled with tears. Amelia was a great listener, and Jeanie found herself pouring out her thoughts.

"I just can't believe everything that's happened. They're saying it was terrorists who flew planes into the buildings, and at the Pentagon. I can't believe how the towers collapsed. I can't believe that he's gone," she said, thinking aloud. "What must he have gone through, Amelia? Was he afraid? Was he really killed? Will we ever find his body?"

Amelia suddenly interrupted her with an urgency in her voice: "Jeanie, I've got to tell you something. God gave me a message for you."

Jeanie looked up, surprised. Amelia was a very down-to-earth person, not given to mysterious ways or speaking for God. She could tell by Amelia's intent, serious expression that she was completely sincere. "What is it?"

"I told Peggy, but I wanted to wait until you were ready before I told you. It seems like now is the time," she began quietly. "Jeanie, it was that night, on Sept. 11, and I was crying out to the Lord about Al. I was saying, 'Lord, what has happened to Al? Is he gone? Is he alive?'"

Jeanie sat riveted; she was touched that Amelia had been praying for her husband.

Amelia continued, "All of a sudden, in my mind, I saw angels coming around Al's building while it was burning. They were taking believers home. I knew they would take Al home, too." She continued, "Then He reminded me of Shadrach, Meshach, and Abed-Nego."

Jeanie knew those names: They were the three Hebrew friends of the prophet Daniel in the Old Testament. They would not worship a towering golden idol built by King Nebuchadnezzar, the ruler of Babylon. They said they trusted in Jehovah God, and that they knew He was able to save them from the furnace—whether He chose to or not. They would only worship God. Enraged, the king had them cast into the blazing fiery furnace that was so hot it had scorched and killed the soldiers who threw them in. To his astonishment, the king saw them loosed from their bonds and walking around peacefully—accompanied by a fourth man who resembled the Son of God. The king called them out, and they walked out of the furnace. He and the other leaders *"saw these men on whose bodies the fire had no power; the hair of their head was not singed nor were their garments affected, and the smell of fire was not on them"* (Daniel 3:27b). The only thing that had been burned was their bonds. The pagan king was so impressed that he praised them, allowed them to worship their God, and made a decree forbidding anyone to criticize the Hebrews' God.

"Remember how they weren't burned by the fire?" Amelia said, "Just like those men, Al was not burned. God was showing me that his body was not burned, Jeanie."

Jeanie's eyes were full of tears. She had wondered if he had burned to death. She had wondered about Al's body—would they ever find him? Was he dead or maybe alive somewhere? At that moment she knew that some of her questions had been answered; she felt God confirm to her heart that Amelia's words were from Him.

"I believe what you're saying," Jeanie said, smiling with tears. "It's so comforting. Thank you for sharing it with me." The two women hugged and thanked the Lord for His word of encouragement. They knew that God could have saved Al—his life or his body—from the burning buildings. And Jeanie knew, deep in her soul, that she was going to continue trusting her God no matter what happened.

Meditation

"The hair of their head was not singed nor were their garments affected, and the smell of fire was not on them."
Daniel 3:27b

It is good to remember God's faithfulness in the fire. When your loved one passed on, consider how the Lord was faithful to them or to you. Perhaps they passed with little pain; perhaps they went quickly and unexpectedly. Whatever the circumstances, Jesus was walking with them in their final moments.

Chapter 5

A NEW HOPE

But the path of the just is like the shining sun,
that shines ever brighter unto the perfect day.
Proverbs 4:18

For I, the LORD your God, will hold your right hand,
saying to you, 'Fear not, I will help you.'
Isaiah 41:13

At first, Jeanie wrestled with the hope that Al might still be alive. Different scenarios would come into her mind of ways Al could have survived. Maybe he had been struck on the head, had amnesia, and now was wandering around not knowing who he was. Maybe he was still at Ground Zero, trapped alive in the rubble. Part of her would not give up. She tied yellow ribbons around the trees in the yard and around the outside of the house, representing the hope that Al would return home. Jeanie filled out a "missing person" report with the Middletown Police Department. Family members and friends regularly called area hospitals, posted Al's picture in the city, and sent out emails and requests for any information on his whereabouts.

But as the days wore on, it seemed clearer that Al wasn't coming home. Searchers stopped finding people alive at Ground Zero. Then they stopped finding bodies at all. It became apparent that the force of the buildings' collapse had left little intact. Jeanie's common sense reasoned that Al surely was dead, yet her heart did not want to let go of him. She prayed that God would either give her release from these thoughts or that He would restore Al to her and the children.

One day a grief counselor, Pastor David Cotton from her oldest son's church, came to visit her and talk to all of the family. Meeting with each family member one at a time in a separate room, Pastor David asked Jeanie how she was doing. They talked a bit and then he asked, "Jeanie, when are you going to plan Al's memorial service?"

Jeanie didn't meet his gaze. "Oh, I figured I'll bury him when they find his body," she said.

He asked gently, "Jeanie, what if they don't find his body? What if it takes years, and you still never have his body?" Jeanie didn't say anything, and he continued: "Don't you think that you—all of you— should have some closure?"

There it was, the question she had suppressed for days: Was she ready to accept that Al was gone? Was she ready to let him go? She knew that they may never find his body—it had likely been crushed in the tons of metal and concrete. And Al had been so high up, on the 104th floor, making the reality of finding his body even less plausible.

She sighed and silently prayed, *Lord, please help me. Please show me what to do.* After a few moments, she knew the answer.

"You're right," she said. "Let me talk to my family—to my children and Al's parents—and see what they want to do." She knew that Al would want them all to be in agreement, that a service should be conducted peacefully and not bring more grief to the family.

The family agreed that it was time to have a memorial service for Al. As Jeanie planned the ceremony and made the arrangements, she sensed the Lord leading her. She asked specifically for His direction for the service. *What would Al want for his memorial service?* She thought. *What do You want, Lord?*

As she began to let go of her hope in Al's return, she was reminded of another hope—a hope that the Bible says *"does not disappoint"* (Romans 5:5). It was the hope that she would see Al again in heaven because he had trusted in Christ as his Savior. The eternal hope that she and Al had in Christ could not be diminished by sorrow or mourning. She clung to the knowledge that Al was waiting for her in eternity, where she would also see her Savior, Jesus Christ. The Bracas all believed in God's Word which speaks clearly of the resurrection of those in the faith who died: *"But I do not want you to be ignorant, brethren, concerning those who have fallen asleep, lest you sorrow as others who have no hope. For if we believe that Jesus died and rose again, even so God will bring with Him those who sleep in Jesus"* (1 Thessalonians 4:13-14).

The more Jeanie prayed and contemplated, the more she determined that the ceremony should be a clear witness for Christ. It would not be a dreary event only for tears and mourning; it would be a celebration of Al's life and of their hope in Jesus. Al would have wanted it that way. And Jeanie also desired that God would receive glory and honor. Christ was so much a part of Al's life; He should be honored at Al's death.

As the memorial service neared, one day there was a knock at the door. It was Ray and Vivian Fagin. Ray introduced himself as an assistant pastor at CC Old Bridge. He said he had come to speak with Jeanie in private, and he held a piece of paper in his hand.

As they stood in Jeanie's kitchen together, Ray said, "I have something to show you, Jeanie."

"OK," she said, sensing from his tone that it was something significant and serious. *Oh Lord, please help me receive this news. Give me Your grace.*

"We've been hearing through emails that, on 9/11, Al was in a conference room. He had lots of people gathered around him, and he was comforting them, and talking to them about the Lord," the man said, gesturing to the paper in his hand.

Jeanie blinked. She tried to picture Al at the Cantor Fitzgerald offices—the plane having hit a few floors below, his part of the building on fire, the rooms getting hotter and hotter around them—praying with his colleagues who had once teased him for his faith. Could it be true? "What does it say?" she asked.

Ray handed her the paper. Her heart began to beat faster as she read the words. A woman had emailed to relay a phone call that she had received from her husband, who worked with Al and was trapped on the 104th floor with him and their colleagues. Her husband told her that that she should not worry because Al Braca was talking to them about heaven and was comforting them. Al was praying with people, preparing them to meet their Maker.

Jeanie looked up from reading the paper, tears pouring down her face. "Thank God!" she said. "Thank God that He was using him there!"

She remembered how Al had wanted to leave his job several times but always felt that God wanted him to stay a little longer because his spiritual work there wasn't finished. She thought about all the nights that Al had come home, grieved by the sins of his coworkers, telling her story after story about how he knew that they needed Christ. Many of them teased him for his faith and his values. Despite their public ridicule, many of them would come to Al privately about their broken marriages and other sorrows. She remembered his compassion for them. He had always prayed for them, had always taken the time to listen and to share with them. Jeanie and Al had prayed together countless times for his coworkers and had felt God's love for them.

"No wonder God never let him leave there; He knew he needed to stay," Jeanie said, her voice barely a whisper. "Maybe a lot of people came to the Lord in those last few minutes." She felt a new sense of peace. So many nights since 9/11 she had wondered why God would allow Al to be taken—why He hadn't kept Al home that day and spared his life. Now she had an answer. God had used Al in a mighty way; He had put him there for that moment—"for such a time as this," as the Book of Esther says.

Instead of hoping that Al would be found alive, she had a new hope: That his death had not been in vain. God had used him to share the message of the Gospel in his final moments. Her heart thrilled to think that maybe some of Al's coworkers had accepted Christ as their Savior and would spend eternity in heaven instead of hell. *God knows,* she thought.

Other reports came in that Al had been holding hands and praying with coworkers before the towers collapsed. Jeanie rejoiced in these reports, thanking God. *Lord, You are so good. You are confirming this hope, that it is true—that Al really was serving You this way before he died. Thank You, Jesus.*

Meditation

For I, the LORD your God, will hold your right hand, saying to you, 'Fear not, I will help you.'
Isaiah 41:13

Whatever you are facing today, God will help you. Just lift your hand to Him, and He will take your hand. Whatever decisions, emotions, or circumstances you face, He will help you. Just ask Him; He is listening.

Chapter 6

A PROPHESY FULFILLED

"Behold, I have given him for a witness to the people."
Isaiah 55:4a

A few days after 9/11, Jeanie was sleeping when her friend Peggy Cuozzo excitedly shook her awake. Jeanie and Al had been friends for years with Peggy and Gary Cuozzo, a former NFL football player who loved the Lord. Their son Jeff Cuozzo was overseas, serving on the mission field in England, and Peggy had been talking to him on the phone that morning. After she hung up with Jeff, she had come straight over to Jeanie's to share the news.

Her eyes sparkling with joy, Peggy asked, "Jeanie! Do you remember how someone had prophesied over Al that he would spread the Gospel around the world?"

Jeanie paused to remember: Earlier that year, she and Al had been on vacation in the Bahamas. When they attended a service at a small church in Nassau, the pastor's wife had prophesied that Al would be instrumental in bringing the Gospel to the world—through TV, newspapers, and radio. At the time, Al and Jeanie could only wonder what it meant. Now the memory came flooding back to her.

"Yes," Jeanie said, coming closer.

Peggy recounted excitedly: "Well, someone from the BBC found out that Jeff knew Al. They called him and were interviewing him live on the radio and asking questions about Al. He got to share the Gospel, Jeanie—on the air! Usually they aren't allowed to discuss Jesus Christ so openly, but he spent the whole hour talking about Al and how he was a Christian. He said it was a miracle!"

They rejoiced together that the Gospel had gone out to listeners all over the UK. The prophetic word from the pastor in Nassau was coming true: the Lord was using Al's life for His glory, to share the

Gospel with the lost around the world. Jeanie felt a joy that plumbed the depth of her grief. Even though Al was not here with her, at least his death had not been in vain.

Meditation

"Behold, I have given him for a witness to the people."
Isaiah 55:4a

God can use even the sorrows and loss that we experience to shine through our lives, to be a witness and a testimony to others who are lost or hurting. Ask Him to open a door for you to share the hope of Christ with someone through the loss you have experienced. The time will come; He will open that door, and you will simply speak the truth of God into someone's life.

Chapter 7

GOD BRINGS RESOLUTION

I waited patiently for the LORD;
and he inclined unto me, and heard my cry.
Psalm 40:1

The LORD will give strength to His people;
the LORD will bless His people with peace.
Psalm 29:11

As she was planning the memorial service, Jeanie wanted to share the news that Al had died honoring God. Someone commented that Al may not have stayed behind with his coworkers but rather had jumped to his death from the 104th floor like so many other terrified victims that day. Perhaps this was why they had not found his body, the person said. Jeanie tried to dismiss the nasty thought, but it ate at her. *Lord, what can I say to that? I can't prove that Al didn't jump. But I know he didn't; he stayed with those people until the end.*

A week after 9/11, she had her answer. That morning, Greg and David had taken some of Al's belongings with DNA to a medical examiner working with the 9/11 recovery.

While they were gone, Peggy Cuozzo pulled up in front of the Braca home. She saw police officers ready to go into Jeanie's house and quickly intercepted them before they reached the door. As she suspected, they had news about Al, and Peggy asked them to let her break the news to Jeanie since she had a heart condition.

Inside the house, Peggy urged Jeanie to sit down with her to receive the news. "Jeanie," she said softly, "What have we been praying for?"

"A miracle," Jeanie answered slowly.

"Well, Jeanie, you have your miracle: They found Al's body," Peggy said, watching Jeanie's reaction closely. "Sunday, when you have the memorial service, you can have total closure, because they found his body."

Jeanie could hardly believe it. *How did You do it, Lord?* Instead of a heavy sadness, she felt relief and gratitude fill her heart. "Praise the Lord," she said, hugging Peggy.

A few moments later, the two police officers walked in to deliver the news in person to Jeanie. One officer began soberly, "Mrs. Braca, we have some news for you."

"I know; thank You, Jesus!" Jeanie said with emotion.

The officer's face went white. "No, ma'am, you don't understand. We found your husband's body."

"I know! Praise God," Jeanie replied. The man looked confused.

Quickly she explained the gratefulness and release that she was feeling: "You see, it's an answer to our prayers. If we never found his body, we would keep looking for him for the rest of our lives. We would swear he was still alive, just lost somewhere with amnesia or something. We would have no peace. But God has given us peace today."

She felt the Holy Spirit filling her heart and mind with a new peace. God had given her an answer; He had given them another miracle.

About 20 minutes later, Jeanie's son David and her son-in-law Greg came in bursting with the same news, explaining how events had unfolded. They had taken samples of Al's DNA to a medical examiner in order to try to identify whether any fragments of Al's body may have been found in the wreckage at the Twin Towers site.

When they arrived, they were taken into a private room and the medical examiner started asking them questions, to their surprise. They told the story together: "They described Dad completely—they asked us, 'Did he have a jeep? White hair? Brown pants? A yellow golf shirt? Did he have a ring that said inside, "To AB love JB"?' We said 'Yes,

yes.' They told us they had found him." David finished earnestly, "It was him, mom."

Waves of relief and sadness surged through all of them: They had finally found Al's body and could stop their search. At the same time, the reality fell upon each one of them that Al was truly dead. They began to cry and hug each other.

That afternoon, Jeanie took down the yellow ribbons from the trees in the yard. The search was over. They could lay Al's body to rest at last.

Later that night when she went to bed, Jeanie remembered how Amelia had shared her vision of Shadrach, Meshach, and Abed-Nego. God had told Amelia that Al's body had not been burned. Now Jeanie had proof: God had been with her beloved Al up until the very end. Al had not been frightened but had been full of faith, sharing the Gospel. He had not jumped from a window; he never felt the pain of the flames. God had truly held him in His hand all the way to the end. "Thank You, Jesus," she whispered. She felt both sadness and resolution in finally letting go of the hope that Al was still alive. But she was greatly comforted by knowing that he had not suffered. She was so proud of her husband; what a legacy he had left behind for their children! *That's my Al,* she thought as she drifted to sleep. *He is home with the Lord. I just know God said to him, 'Well done, My good and faithful servant.'*

Meditation

The LORD will give strength to His people;
the LORD will bless His people with peace.
Psalm 29:11

If you are waiting for resolution from the loss of your loved one, you can ask God to help you. He will bring you peace and closure; lean on Him and ask Him to help you. He will.

Chapter 8

REMEMBERING AL

As iron sharpens iron, so a man sharpens the countenance of his friend. ...
And a man is valued by what others say of him.
Proverbs 21:17, 21b

On the brisk morning of Sunday, September 23, a small group of family and friends gathered at Fair View Cemetery in Middletown, NJ, to pray and worship God. Al's casket rested on top of the ground. Jeanie's pastor, Bruce Koczman of Calvary Chapel Four Winds spoke to the group as his wife Karen played acoustic guitar and led the group in singing worship songs. Jeanie sang softly and fervently with tears in her eyes.

She had never expected this day to come, but now that it was here, she wanted it to serve a higher purpose than just mourning. She wanted both to celebrate Al's life and to point all who attended to their Savior, Jesus Christ. She knew Al was in heaven because he had followed Jesus. She didn't want anyone to leave without knowing Christ.

To accommodate a large gathering, the family held the indoor service at Tower Hill First Presbyterian Church in Red Bank, New Jersey. It was a large, traditional church with a tall white tower and stained glass windows. David, Al and Jeanie's firstborn, was a regular member there, and his pastor had offered to let the family hold the service in the spacious sanctuary. It was the same church where Al had given his daughter Deanna away in marriage just a month ago. Today, nearly 700 people packed the church—squeezed in pews and standing in the back—to honor the memory of Alfred J. Braca.

Jeanie thanked the Lord again for giving the blessed closure that her family needed. She looked around the room. The assembly was a mixture of friends from Calvary Chapel, the Presbyterian church, the Pentecostal church where Jeanie and Al had attended many years ago, family members, friends from their Irish and Italian communities in

Monmouth County, NJ, and people Al had known through his work at Cantor-Fitzgerald.

Many were red-eyed, wiping tears with somber faces. It had been less than two weeks since 9/11, and most local people were still in shock over the attacks. In the local communities, some people had returned to their faith in Christ. Many others, shaken by the tragedy, seemed more open to God now than they ever had been. Jeanie wondered if any of them would soften their hearts toward Christ today.

She looked at the program for the memorial service. The pastor's wife, Karen Koczman, had lovingly worked with Jeanie to put together a special program for Al. Several pages long, it was filled with pictures of Al, their family, and Scripture verses. Each of the children had written a note about Al—favorite memories or qualities that they treasured most. Jeanie wrote that his "heart was wholly given to God." Christopher wrote that his dad was his hero, that Al had often told his son that he loved him, and died "in honor and dignity." Deanna recalled her father's love and dedication to his family, and that he taught her "to trust God and walk in faith." Christina recounted "him loving me and accepting me through God's unconditional love." David wrote, "Throughout my own struggles with faith and grace…he always listened, encouraged, and prayed with me."

On the last page, they had included the lyrics to Al's favorite song, "The Lighthouse," while a family friend sang the song.

The chorus read,

> *And I thank God for the lighthouse;*
> *I owe my life to Him.*
> *Oh Jesus is the Lighthouse*
> *And from the rocks of sin*
> *He has shone the light around me*
> *That I could clearly see.*
> *If it wasn't for the Lighthouse,*
> *Tell me, where would this ship be?*

Inside the booklet, they had included Al's letter from God that Jeanie had found on September 12 in his Bible. On the second page of the program was Al's favorite Scripture:

> *Trust in the LORD with all your heart,*
> *And lean not on your own understanding;*
> *In all your ways acknowledge Him,*
> *And He shall direct your paths.* Proverbs 3:5-6, NKJV

As she read the familiar verse, it took on a new meaning for her. She would continue to trust the Lord, and wanted others to as well. She prayed silently that those who did not know Christ as their Savior would be touched by the verses, by Al's legacy, and by the Spirit of the Lord. She prayed that today they would trust in their Lord with all of their hearts.

This ceremony also started with songs of worship to God. First, they sang "Shout to the Lord."

> *My Jesus, my Savior, Lord there is none like You*
> *All of my days I want to praise the wonders of Your mighty love*
> *My comfort, my shelter, tower of refuge and strength*
> *Let every breath, all that I am, never cease to worship You*

As she set her mind on Jesus, Jeanie felt God's presence as she had so many times before over the last two weeks. She stood up and lifted her hands to God. It was as if everything else melted away, and she was standing before the Lord—just her and Jesus. She praised God, acknowledging Him as almighty and in control. She felt His love for her. She prayed silently, *God, give me Your strength to make it through this day and to walk in Your purpose—whatever You want to do through me today, have Your way.*

Pastors spoke about Al's life, how he had lived for God and often had shared the Word and the Gospel with others. They shared about God's comfort and encouraged people to have a close relationship with the Lord as Al had done.

Then Tom Parello got up to speak. He had been Al's best friend, and their children often called him "Uncle Tom." Jeanie had known his wife, Maria, since she was 14 years old. Both couples had married around the same time, and from the first time they had shared a meal together, Al and Tom had become fast friends. The Parellos had also become Christians, and the four of them would often get together to talk, fellowship, pray, or go on weekend trips and vacations together.

Jeanie remembered how their trips would usually start: Al and Tom would be in the front seats while Jeanie, Maria, and sometimes their youngest son, Christopher, would sit in the back. Maria would often say, "OK, Al, you're in charge of the music ministry." And Al would laugh and pull out his Christian music tapes. But before they would go very far, Al would always say, "Let's pray." Then he would ask God to bless their conversation and fellowship—that they would encourage each other in the Lord and build each other up in their mutual faith.

Sharing from the stage that day, Tom recalled a similar memory: "We never went anywhere without Al praying first. Even if it was just riding around. He was such an example to me. I was honored, so touched, at Deanna's wedding a few months ago when he introduced me to his coworkers as his brother. That was something we always knew but never said. I thank God for that."

Tom stopped to steady his voice. "Al was the best friend I've ever had. The friendship we had was like the godly love it talks about in 1 Corinthians 13—we were never envious of each other; we always had patience with each other. He always helped bring me closer to the Lord—who could ask for a better friend than that?"

Jeanie nodded, tears flowing down her face. She remembered one day when Tom and Maria had come over for coffee. After they all sat down, Al told Tom, "I feel that God showed me that you are going to speak in tongues tonight." Jeanie was surprised; Al didn't say such things lightly or often.

She was even more surprised when Tom replied, "Isn't that amazing? I had that same thought today! I've never spoken in tongues before—never even had the desire to—but I felt like God showed me that tonight I would." The Parellos and the Bracas both believed in the spiritual gifts mentioned in the Bible but did not go to churches that over-emphasized those gifts or pressured people to experience them. That night, as the four of them prayed together in the Bracas' home, Tom was filled with the Holy Spirit and spoke in tongues. The four of them had rejoiced at sharing such a special moment together.

Then the mother of Greg Cambeis, Jeanie's son-in-law, stood up to share. Mary Ann Cambeis talked about how she had raised Greg as a single mom and how Al had reached out to the young man when he was a teenager. "Al was like a father to him—even before Greg married Christina," she said.

Jeanie's thoughts drifted to when she and Al first met Greg. A 16-year-old with a mohawk, the stocky, dark-haired young man had a crush on their daughter and began coming around the Bracas' home in Middletown. Greg was a party kid. Even though Al did not want his daughter to get deeply involved with this young man, Al couldn't help but also see that Greg needed a father. He needed someone to show him what a godly man was; most of all, he needed Christ. So when Greg would come to the house, Al would talk to him.

One night, Al saw that Greg had gotten drunk and passed out in someone's yard, so he hoisted him up and took him home. The next time Greg came over, Al told him, "If you want to date my daughter, you're going to have to straighten up and fly right. No more drinking and partying. That's not how I raised Christina." By this time, Al had built such a rapport with Greg that the young man listened to him with respect.

It wasn't very long after that when Greg accepted Christ as his Savior. As he came to church with them and turned his back on his old lifestyle, Greg began to grow in the Lord. Finally, a few years after they first met him, he asked Al for Christina's hand in marriage. Having watched Greg grow into a godly young man, Al happily gave his consent.

Jeanie glanced over at Greg. She didn't think of him as her son-in-law, but as one of her own sons. Now Greg and Christina had two beautiful children; they were a family who loved the Lord. What an impact Al had made on their lives. What a difference the Lord had made in Greg through Al's love, patience, and gentle sharing of the truth. Jeanie looked around the room, seeing face after face of those whose lives had been touched by Al.

Remembering the way Al had lived and his faith in the Lord was like a light of hope in such a dark time. *Thank You, Jesus. Thank You that You aren't done impacting people through Al's life,* she thought. That day, she could not have foreseen how God would continue that ministry through her in the coming months.

Another woman shared a story: One of Al's coworkers had gotten a message through to his family that Al was praying with several of them while the building was still burning. Jeanie smiled, thanking God for so many reports that confirmed the same story. She hoped some of the coworkers he had prayed with that day were now in heaven with him. The entire room was silent as people listened with amazement, many of them weeping and quietly rejoicing.

After the service, people filtered over to Webster Hall for refreshments and dessert. Jeanie and her children stood in a line shaking hands and thanking people for coming. One man, Rick Burman, introduced himself as the coworker who had given Al the nickname "The Rev." At the time, the nickname had been a way to tease Al for his Christian beliefs; today, Rick's face was serious as he spoke with respect about their father being a good man.

Jeanie didn't know if anyone had accepted Christ as their Lord and Savior that day, but she knew that the Gospel had been presented— not only through the Scriptures and speakers, but through Al's life. He truly had been a light in a dark place, and she felt that his light was still shining.

"Let your light so shine before men, that they may see your good works and glorify your Father in heaven." Matthew 5:16

Like the glow of a sunset after the sun has vanished over the horizon, so Al's love for the Lord was still a light to others—even after his death.

Meditation

Trust in the LORD with all your heart,
And lean not on your own understanding;
In all your ways acknowledge Him,
And He shall direct your paths.
Proverbs 3:5-6, NKJV

As you walk this journey of grieving or going on without your loved one, trust in the Lord. Whatever decisions or crossroads you come to, stop and invite Him into the situation through prayer; ask Him to direct your paths. He will guide you on this strange new journey.

Chapter 9

ANOTHER CEREMONY

Rejoice with those who rejoice, and weep with those who weep.
Romans 12:15

Jesus wept. Then the Jews said, "See how He loved him!"
John 11:35-36

A few days after the memorial service, Jeanie returned with David and Greg to the place where they had talked to the Red Cross to help identify Al's body—a warehouse on 92nd Street in Manhattan. This time, Jeanie was to be given a flag to honor Al as a victim of 9/11. Of the roughly 2,800 victims that died at Ground Zero, less than half would ever be positively identified by physical remains. More than 1,600 people were issued death certificates without any remains ever being found.

In silence, the three of them rode side by side in the back of a limousine that Jeanie had hired for that day. She had guessed it would be an emotional experience and that they would want the privacy. There were bound to be press people or strangers around; she wanted to have a place near at hand where they could quickly be alone.

This is my first time going into the city since it happened, Jeanie thought to herself. Always, the city had been her stomping ground—filled with her memories as a girl, a teenager, and a newly married young woman. She and Al had walked these streets together years ago when they were dating. Now it all seemed foreign to her, like a different world. As they neared Manhattan, the scenery changed from normal city bustle to eerily deserted streets. Finally, the sleek black car turned from Lexington Avenue onto East 92nd Street. They were close to where the East River and the Harlem River converged. All was quiet. It seemed as if all busyness and work and life had stopped.

When they got inside the large building, they were taken to a back room to fill out numerous forms. Since that infamous day, it seemed like mountainous piles of paperwork met Jeanie at every turn. On her dining room table, making their own strange skyline, piles of forms waited for her, constantly growing taller as new ones were added weekly. A few hours later, after all of the forms had been filled out, the three of them were solemnly ushered to a tent filled with NYC police officers.

Jeanie was shown to a spot where an American Flag was folded in Al's honor and given to her. Jeanie, David, and Greg watched as the two police officers gravely folded the flag with tears streaming down their faces. The man and woman wore blue uniforms adorned with medals. Though highly decorated and experienced officers, they were obviously touched by seeing the faces of the victim's family.

Another service. Another reminder that Al is gone. Another token of what happened, Jeanie thought silently. She was grateful for the gesture, but it brought wrenching emotions to a wound that was still too fresh. She took the flag—a blue triangle with white stars folded neatly—and thanked them. It felt heavy in her trembling arms. Jeanie and her two sons walked back to the limousine in silence.

As soon as the chauffer closed the door behind them, the three of them burst into tears. Nobody said much. They all felt emotionally and physically exhausted. Finally Jeanie said, "Boys, are you hungry? Would you like to eat dinner with me?" She wanted to feed them, to comfort them, to strengthen them after such a long day.

They went to a nice Italian restaurant and sat down. Jeanie said, "Order whatever you want. Let's just leave it behind us—what happened today. Let's just relax and have a nice meal together." They agreed. As they ate, they talked about family things and Jeanie's grandchildren. No one mentioned 9/11 or the Towers or terrorists or the memorial service. Jeanie felt a small relief as they set their mind on the present and left behind the past—at least for a little while.

Meditation

Jesus wept. Then the Jews said, "See how He loved him!"
John 11:35-36

Jesus wept when Lazarus died, even though He knew that He would raise him from the dead. The loss of a loved one brings sorrow. Sometimes we need to weep—whether alone or together with others who loved that person. Allow yourself time to weep. It is not weak or faithless to weep for a departed loved one; even Jesus did.

Chapter 10

HELP FROM AFAR

And the LORD shall help them and deliver them…
and save them, because they trust in Him.
Psalm 37:40

That fall was filled with changes, of trying to find a new normal, of trying to learn to live on her own. Jeanie was trying to find her footing and adjust to life without her husband, her spiritual covering—the one who had looked out for her welfare, the one who had led them as he felt led by God. She had never had to make major decisions without Al before. She felt alone and uncertain. She knew that she needed to trust in God, but she wished she had someone to talk to about her burdens and other decisions that were cropping up. She didn't want to trouble her children with such things—not now, not when they were having a hard enough time dealing with their own grief and adjusting to life without their beloved father.

God brought people at just the right moments to help with all of the details. Jeanie had always left the finances up to Al. Now there were bills to pay and mounds of paperwork to sort out. Her friend Gary Cuozzo was helping her pay bills until Al's life insurance money came in. Her close friend Mary Jane Behan came to visit her; she helped Jeanie open a bank account and learn how to write a check. God continued to bring people to help Jeanie through this new season of her life.

She saw the Lord's fingerprints in all of the details. Judy Tier helped Jeanie decorate their new house and worked with her to organize the multiple legal and financial appointments she had to sort out paperwork. Several of her sisters in Christ from CC Four Winds stepped in to love her through her grief. They kept her busy, spending time with her so that she didn't have to be alone as her family returned to their jobs and their lives. Cathy Edelman, Jackie Larson and Peggy took Jeanie shopping, made sure she ate regular meals, and went to Bible study with her. Their kindness and love gave her strength. Bernedette House, also a nurse, came over every day to check Jeanie's blood pressure and her heart to make sure her health did not deteriorate. Jeanie felt the Lord loving her through them. Even though she was no longer part of a couple, she was not utterly alone. The body of Christ came around her in a tangible, loving way as God's arms of love.

Others from outside the church reached out to Jeanie. At the end of September 2001, one day Jeanie received a phone message. A man's gentle voice said, "Hello Jeanie, I got your number from a pastor at Calvary Chapel Old Bridge. My name is Pastor Jim Misiuk from Calvary Chapel Lake Forest, CA. We asked if there were any families they knew who might have some needs because of the tragedy. They gave us your name, and we'd like to help."

Jeanie called Pastor Jim back to thank him. As they talked, he explained that his church in Southern California wanted to reach out specifically to believers who had been affected by 9/11. "We'd like to help any way we can—financially, spiritually—whatever you need. We're here to support you in any way. We want you to know you're not alone, that we're here for you. And we'd like to be here for the long term because we understand that this will be a long process," he said. "My wife Mary Ann and I are available to pray for whatever you need. You can call us any time, for anything."

Jeanie listened to him. She was amazed at the Lord's provision: He knew that she needed extra prayer support. She talked to him a bit longer about her family, his church, and his offer to be available for prayer.

"I just want God to get glory from this," Jeanie said. She had kept that desire in focus every day, trying to make decisions that would please the Lord. That was the motivation that helped her to get out of bed in the morning, in every conversation she had, in every decision she made.

"We'll pray for that," Jim said. "What else can we pray for?"

Jeanie gave some general requests for herself and her family, and then Jim prayed for her. His tone was gentle and compassionate. She could tell that he had the gift of encouragement, and she sensed God's Spirit behind his words.

"Do you mind if I keep calling you and praying with you through this?" he offered. "I know you'll need prayer as different things come up." She agreed, and he and his wife began calling Jeanie once or twice a week, always asking how she and her family were doing and praying for her on the phone. The church sent Jeanie and Christopher some money to help until the financial settlements worked out. Jeanie saw it as God's hand providing for their practical needs—that a church she had never visited, all the way on the West Coast would contact them and offer support.

That year, and continuing over the next decade, Jeanie would often call Pastor Jim and Mary Ann when things came up for which she needed prayer or guidance from the Lord. Many times, they would simply listen as she shared her feelings or a situation that had come up. They would always pray with her, and often God would later show Jeanie the answer that she needed. Sometimes they would offer practical advice. Jeanie thanked God for hand-picking a pair of friends for her when she needed them most—a brother and sister in Christ whom she could lean on. *God, You continue to amaze me,* she often thought.

Meditation

*And the LORD shall help them and deliver them
…and save them, because they trust in Him.*
Psalm 37:40

As you adjust to life without your loved one, you may need help filling in the gaps or the small details without them. It is all right to ask someone for help. If you don't know who to ask, then ask the Lord. He will help you because you trust in Him.

Chapter 11

A CALL FROM AL

For there is not a word on my tongue, but behold, O LORD, You know it altogether. You have hedged me behind and before, and laid Your hand upon me. Psalm 139:4-5

Nearly a month after Al's death, Jeanie heard his last words.

An MCI operator called the house while she was out. Christina was visiting and answered the phone. The operator, Wilma, said she had urgent news about Al. She had been on the phone with him on 9/11 and heard his last words, a message for his family. Christina listened to the details. When Jeanie came home, Christina told her that an operator had called with a message from Al.

Jeanie's heart began to race. It had been nearly a month since he died—for weeks she had been wondering what his final thoughts were, what his final words had been. Had he been afraid? Did he know he was going to die? Did he think about her or the children? What was on his mind in his last moments?

Christina told her the brief message that the operator had relayed.

"I want to call her," Jeanie said.

Christina hesitated. "I don't think you should; it might upset you."

Jeanie felt a peace from the Lord. For the past few weeks, she had been drawing closer to the Lord, and she felt His presence protecting her. She felt as if He were literally holding her together—her heart, her mind, her health. She knew it would be all right to call. Christina dialed the number for her.

Jeanie introduced herself as the wife of Al Braca. The older woman responded, "My name is Wilma, and I'm an operator for MCI. I received a phone call from Mr. Braca on September 11—he gave me a message for you. I am sorry it has taken me so long to find you." She explained that Al had been unable to dial out from the phones at his offices but had placed an emergency operator call.

"Go on," Jeanie said.

Wilma shared the message as closely to Al's actual words as possible. As she spoke, her voice became heavy with emotion:"He said, 'Wilma, help me. I feel like my feet are on fire. I'm not going to make it. Will you please contact my family and tell them that I love them? Tell my wife Jeanie and my children that I love them. Tell them not to worry.'" Wilma had stayed on the phone with him until the line went dead.

Tears were streaming down Jeanie's cheeks. Those were Al's words; she could almost hear his voice saying them. His last words had been for her, for their children. He had told her not to worry—she was sure that the Holy Spirit had been giving him peace and clarity, helping him deal with his impending death. She thanked Wilma. Wilma told Jeanie that she had been touched by her conversation with Al and asked Jeanie to send her a picture of him. Knowing she was the last person to talk to him had made a deep impact on the woman. *That was the kind of man Al was,* Jeanie thought. *He made an impact on every soul he touched.*

Hanging up the phone, Jeanie praised the Lord. *God, You are so good. You are so good to get that message to me now, when I need to hear it the most. Thank you for being with Al right to the end, holding his hand, giving him courage. He felt the heat of the flames, but You didn't allow his body to be burned. Praise You, Father. You are so good.*

When Christopher came home, she sat him down and related the entire message to him. He had tears in his eyes too, but he was glad to hear that his dad's last thoughts had been about his family. Jeanie told each of their other children, who all had a similar reaction. To know their father's final words was a great comfort.

A few months later, Christopher talked to Christin Ditchfield with *Focus on the Family Magazine* about his father's phone call: "The last thing my dad did involved the two things most important to him—God and his family. He loved to lead people to Christ. That takes away a lot of the hurt and the pain."

Hearing Al's last words had meant the world to Jeanie and her family; she thanked God for another miraculous gift in the wake of his passing.

———————————

Meditation

A man is valued by what others say of him.
Proverbs 27:21b

What legacy did your loved one leave behind? How did they help people? Protect, teach, serve? Did they share words of wisdom? Shine for Jesus? It is good to remember and cherish their legacy.

Chapter 12

SHARING A NEW MESSAGE

Listen, for I will speak of excellent things,
and from the opening of my lips will come right things;
for my mouth will speak truth.
Proverbs 8:6-7a

I can do all things through Christ who strengthens me.
Philippians 4:13

Jeanie sensed the Lord leading her through each day. She was trusting Him daily and staying in the Word. Friends and family were constantly listening, encouraging, and praying for her. She was interviewed several times, and Al's story was featured in several magazines and news outlets—both Christian and secular. Letters of consolation and encouragement poured in from people around the world. Many told her that Al's valor and faith in the face of death had given them fresh courage to live for Christ.

The whirlwind of paperwork dwindled to a steady stream, and the memorial service had brought a sense of closure. One morning in November, the telephone rang. It was Sue, the principal of a Christian school in New Brunswick where Jeanie's daughter Deanna taught. Sue invited Jeanie to speak to the students on Veterans Day—exactly two months after the attacks. Jeanie said she would pray about it.

Jeanie never liked the spotlight. Al was always the brave one—the one who had quiet strength, who could handle pressure, who gave "a word fitly spoken" (Proverbs 25:11) for people when they needed it. She enjoyed sharing with people one-on-one, but could she stand before a whole crowd and talk about the biggest heartbreak of her life? "Lord, how can I go talk to these children about what happened? What will I say?" Jeanie asked, reluctantly. She knew that, in her own strength, she could never do it. But God had given her His strength before. She bowed her head in surrender and prayed, "Lord, if You want me to do this, I will. Just give me peace so that I know it's from You."

She had learned to ask God all of her questions and then wait for Him to answer. Sitting quietly and looking around their now-silent home, Jeanie let treasured memories of Al fill her mind. He had planned in retirement to open a pizzeria in order to reach out to young people. She remembered him saying, "If we can just get them at a young age to really hear about Jesus—who He is, how much He loves them—that would make such a difference!"

She spoke aloud to God, "Is this what You want, Lord? For me to reach out to others, to tell them about Jesus, and to tell them about how Al lived for You?" Jeanie felt a peaceful sense that, if anyone opened the door for her to share, she would go—as a witness for Christ and to carry on Al's legacy. She called Sue back and accepted the invitation.

As she read her Bible and prayed about what to share, she thought about how, since the attacks, she had heard people openly saying "God bless America" in schools and on TV. People were filling churches, praying for their country and mourning. Many people seemed to be turning to God; it appeared that a revival was sweeping the country. One day while she was praying, she had asked, "Lord, what's going on? Will it last?" She had felt Him say it would not last. "Why, Lord?" she had inquired. Because of pride, she felt Him say.

She sensed that He was going to give her a special message to share with people: How He would do a true and lasting work in their lives. *Lord, I've never spoken in front of anyone before,* she thought. *What am I going to say? These are just children.* She felt as if the Lord said, "Just give them My Word." Then she took out a pen and began writing down the verses and thoughts that the Lord put on her mind. They were things He had been showing her in her personal time alone with him—how she could stay close to Him and depend on Him.

A few days later, she was ready to deliver her message. At Cornerstone Christian School in Brunswick, New Jersey, Jeanie stood before a packed assembly hall of boys and girls from preschool through 8th grade. It was Veteran's Day—exactly two months since the towers fell. The principal, Sue, had introduced Jeanie as "the widow of Al Braca, a man who died in the World Trade Center attacks." The children looked expectantly at Jeanie with wide eyes.

"Good morning, boys and girls. Thank you for letting me come share with you," she said. After telling them a little about herself, Jeanie took a deep breath and began to share the special message that she felt God had given her:

"God gave me the acronym of P.R.I.D.E. The first letter is P for Pray. In 1 Thessalonians 5:17, the Word says those of us who are believers are to *pray without ceasing.*' In Psalm 51, there is a prayer of repentance," she said. "In order for God to hear our prayers, we must be born again. The most important prayer we can ever pray is to ask Jesus into our hearts. That's when we're saved."

Next, the letter R stood for "Read the Scriptures." She read 2 Timothy 3:16 which says, *"All Scripture is given by inspiration of God, and is profitable for doctrine, for reproof, for correction, for instruction in righteousness."*

Then she read Psalm 119:105: *"Your word is a lamp to my feet and a light to my path."* She told them that God's word had helped her every day since Al's death; it was a light for her in a dark time.

"The letter 'I'—we must be *'imitators of God as dear children'* as it says in Ephesians 5:1," she said. "We need to walk in love like Christ loved us. We can't imitate this world—dress like the world, talk like the world, live like the world. That will lead us to death. We need to decide: Am I going to have one foot in the world and one foot in church, or am I going to totally surrender to the will of God? Am I going to say as Jesus did, 'Not my will but Your will'?" To keep from having a prideful heart, a person must surrender to God. She added, "No matter what happens to us—even when we have that pain and suffering that comes—we need to surrender to God. He is going to guide us through it, step by step."

She paused, letting her words echo into the silence. Indeed, she had walked with God through the pain and suffering of the past eight weeks. She hoped the children could see that she was sincere, and that this truth was also real for them.

"The 'D' stands for 'Doing' our devotions every day and being *'Doers of the Word, and not hearers only'* like it says in James 1:22," she said. "If we go to church week after week, and hear someone else teach, and never apply it to our lives, we're not going to grow. And when trials and tribulations come our way, we're going to fall flat on our faces."

The letter E, she said, stood for "Edifying one another." Believers should comfort each other with the Scriptures. She shared Romans 15:1-6, part of which says, *"For even Christ did not please Himself; but as it is written, 'The reproaches of those who reproached You fell on Me.' For whatever things were written before were written for our learning, that we through the patience and comfort of the Scriptures might have hope. Now may the God of patience and comfort grant you to be like-minded toward one another, according to Christ Jesus, that you may with one mind and one mouth glorify the God and Father of our Lord Jesus Christ* (verses 3-6)."

She added, "Boys and girls, we are here to glorify God. That's why you were put on this earth: to have fellowship with Christ. Your whole life, your whole being should glorify God. Everything you do should be for His glory. Life is not about us."

Jeanie paused, reliving some of her pain and being reminded of God's compassion. She wondered if any of the children had been hurt through the attacks or lost loved ones. She said, "I know sometimes we're in pain, or we get angry. Sometimes we can feel like part of our heart has been ripped away. I never thought in a million years that my husband wouldn't come home. When it happened, I asked God, 'Didn't we do everything right, Lord?' We had Bible studies in our home. I asked God why He hadn't kept Al from going to work that morning." The children's faces were intent, interested.

"But I know that my husband was a man of God. He had a heart like King David—how the Bible says he was a man after God's own heart. It means he always wanted to please God. My husband hated his job, but he knew God had called him to minister to his co-workers, to people on Wall Street. ...When he would read his Bible at work, he would write down the promises that God had given him and share them with us over dinner. He would pray for his coworkers. When we prayed together, he would say, 'God, I will serve You no matter how unhappy I am; I will be there for these men and women.'"

She told them Al had earned the nickname "the Rev" at work and was often teased for his faith. She shared how she and Al had prayed so many times for the men and women at the Cantor Fitzgerald office, and how she had heard reports that Al had prayed with his coworkers before they died.

She added, "Only God knows if someone gave their life to Him that morning."

For the children who had already committed their lives to Christ, she encouraged them to live for the Lord and to be bold in sharing the Gospel. For those who had not made that personal commitment, she encouraged them to accept Jesus as their Savior—that way they would be ready at any time to meet the Lord in heaven. "One minute your world can be one way, and another minute it's not. The way the World Trade Center came tumbling down that day, my life changed in a just a second."

The children were in rapt attention. Finally, Jeanie closed in prayer, asking God to help them live for Him even in difficult times.

When she went home that day, Jeanie felt a reassurance in her heart that she had been obedient. Her daughter Deanna told her later that all of the children had seemed deeply impacted by her testimony: Students were quieter, more thoughtful during the day, some asking questions. Teachers had approached Deanna to tell her how much Jeanie's message had meant to them.

"Praise the Lord!" Jeanie said. She recalled Philippians 4:13, *"I can do all things through Christ who strengthens me."* The Lord had given her His strength to share honestly with the children. She had no idea how the Lord would continue opening doors for her to share that message over the next few years and touch many lives through her obedience.

———

Meditation

Listen, for I will speak of excellent things,
and from the opening of my lips will come right things;
for my mouth will speak truth.
Proverbs 8:6-7a

Depending on where you are in your journey, God may have a message for you to share with others. Death tends to get people's attention, and they may be open to hearing about heaven or the Gospel as never before.

I can do all things through Christ who strengthens me.
Philippians 4:13

If you are nervous or unsure what to share, ask God to open doors and use you in His timing. As He guides you, you can do all things through Christ who strengthens you.

Chapter 13

MOURNING
WITHOUT BITTERNESS

"The LORD gave, and the LORD has taken away;
Blessed be the name of the LORD."
Job 1:21b

In late November, Jeanie sat in the kitchen talking to Amelia while she ironed. The news was still filled with the devastating effects the tragedy was having on families and friends of the victims. Psychologists were assessing community residents and would soon report that 20 percent of those living near the World Trade Center were suffering from post traumatic stress disorder.[1] In surrounding cities, family members of the victims were experiencing depression, shock, fear, and anger as they tried to get over the loss of a loved one taken violently without warning. Across the country, thousands of Americans were concerned for the future.

In contrast, today Jeanie sat praising God for how He had been speaking to her heart over the last few days. She knew without a doubt that He was with her and was watching over her and her children. "God has been so good to us," she said, with conviction.

Amelia replied, "Jeanie, people are amazed at your faith through all of this—that you're able to get out of bed every day. You're talking about the Lord. You're not bitter or angry at all—not at the terrorists, and not at God."

"Praise God, Amelia," Jeanie said with a slight smile. "My peace comes from Him. I can't be bitter or angry; I have to trust in my Savior."

---

[1] Galea, S., Ahern, J., Resnick, H., Kilpatrick, D., Bucuvalas, M., Gold, J., & Vlahov, D. (2002). Psychological sequelae of the September 11 terrorist attacks in New York City. *New England Journal of Medicine, 346,* 982-987.

She paused. She had paid attention to the stories about other families who lost fathers or mothers. "I have heard that many of the wives are in shock, or on bed rest, or too depressed to get up. They are without hope, but my hope comes from God," she said. She shared about several widows whom she had talked to who were deeply mourning— how she had prayed with them and listened with compassion.

"I pray for them constantly," Jeanie added. And she did. She knew how painful it was to face each new day alone, to face life without her precious husband, and the uncertain climate of a community that had been devastated by death. She knew that, without Christ, she would be lying in bed in the darkness of despair. But His presence and His words were giving her life, every day. He was literally feeding her soul, sustaining her.

A few days later, Amelia asked, "Jeanie, would you and Christopher come to my church and share about what God has been doing in your lives through this?"

Jeanie considered her request. She knew Amelia went to the Tabernacle of Glory in Asbury Park, NJ, where her husband, Joseph Okpanachi, was the senior pastor. He was born in Nigeria and was also the overseer of three churches in Kenya and Nigeria. Jeanie knew that, though they came from different cultures and backgrounds, they all believed in Jesus Christ as their Lord and Savior. She wondered if she and Christopher had anything to say that would be encouraging to the congregation. After praying about it and talking it over with Christopher, they agreed to visit and share.

Sitting on the front row to show their support, all of Jeanie's children and grandchildren had come to hear her and Christopher speak. As she stood before the congregation, a reverent silence filled the room as all eyes were on her. Jeanie's eyes watered, but she didn't weep as she related how she and Al had accepted Christ through Christina's illness, how they had served God together as a family, and how he had died serving Christ in the Twin Towers. He had always been a man of integrity who passionately desired to share the Gospel with his unsaved coworkers and clients. "He was in the belly of the beast in New

York, and he was a light in the midst of darkness," she recalled. After speaking for nearly 40 minutes, she sat down, and her youngest son Christopher stood up to share.

Jeanie watched her son intently. He didn't seem upset; he seemed peaceful. The thoughtful tilt of his head reminded her of Al. Having just turned 16, Christopher was often playful like his father, but this afternoon his face was serious as he began to share. Under his curly dark hair, Chris's dark brown eyes glittered with intensity, as Al's often had when he was talking about God.

"This past summer, before 9/11, I went on a mission trip to Russia," he began. "While I was preparing to go, I was reading my Bible. God really spoke to me through two verses." He read them to the congregation:

"The Lord gave, and the Lord has taken away;
Blessed be the name of the Lord." Job 1:21b

"O Death, where is your sting?
O Hades, where is your victory?" 1 Corinthians 15:55

He continued, "When I first read those, I didn't know why they were so important; I just knew that God was speaking to me. Just a few weeks later, 9/11 happened. Now I understand. I feel like Job—like everything's been stripped away."

Jeanie's heart ached at his words. Losing Al was such a shock for all of them, but Christopher was just a teenager. He had been so close to his father. When Christopher was a little boy, Al had been the Cub Scout leader of his troop for several years. He had looked up to his father in so many ways. On the Labor Day Weekend prior to 9/11, the three of them—Al, Jeanie, and Chris, had gone to Newport, Rhode Island. Some teenagers might have balked at spending a whole weekend with their father, but Christopher had looked forward to it for weeks: His dad had been his hero. As the three of them walked along the port, Jeanie stopped them and took a picture of Al and Christopher. It was their last photo together.

Referring again to the verse in 1 Corinthians, Christopher added, "I know that my dad is with God now. God gave him to me, and God took him home. I know that he's in heaven, and I'll see him again."

Jeanie's eyes welled with tears. She remembered that, right after Christopher had returned from Russia in August, he had shared some of those verses with their fellowship at Calvary Chapel Four Winds, New Jersey. He had spoken about the orphans in Russia and the terrible conditions they endured. He had told the congregation that he wanted to answer the Great Commission that Jesus gave in Matthew 28:19a which says, "Go therefore and make disciples of all the nations." She and Al had looked at each other in surprise, rejoicing together to see their son grow in his faith and responding to God's call.

Today she looked at him with new eyes: Her son was growing into a young man. She thanked God that, instead of becoming bitter, he had also chosen to trust God and draw closer to Christ. She realized that all of the years that she and Al had prayed for Christopher and taught him about the Lord had not been wasted. His faith was becoming his own. She marveled; he had wisdom beyond his years.

As Jeanie and Christopher spoke, the group was extremely quiet. An atmosphere of respect permeated the room among this usually boisterous fellowship. When Christopher sat down, the congregation applauded with zeal. Amelia's husband, Senior Pastor Joseph Okpanachi, thanked them for sharing and encouraging the congregation. Amelia would later tell Jeanie that her own daughters were deeply impacted by Jeanie's joy in the midst of loss and by her daily example of a woman committed to Christ whose actions spoke louder than her words. Members of the fellowship were so encouraged to follow Christ that they talked about Jeanie's and Christopher's testimonies for weeks afterward.

A short time later, when Christopher was invited to speak in public on another occasion, he told Jeanie that he knew the Matthew 28 verse applied to him personally—that he was to go forth and share the Gospel at every opportunity that opened to him because of 9/11. And he did. In the year that followed, he spoke at churches, schools, on television, in magazine and newspaper interviews, and at large public assemblies around New York City. Many people would remark to Jeanie about Christopher's strong faith and his great maturity for his age. She knew that Al would have been proud of his son, who constantly proclaimed how proud he was of his father and his faith in God. Later, her two sons-in-law would also give their testimonies in church.

Meditation

"The LORD gave, and the LORD has taken away;
blessed be the name of the LORD."
Job 1:21b

When we suffer loss and continue to have faith in God, others take notice. It is an amazing witness for Christ. It doesn't mean that we are never sad or that we never question God. Job was horribly grief-stricken, and the book of Job is filled with honest questions of 'why?' Yet it is also filled with Job's faith in His God who gave and had taken away. He refused to curse God; that in itself still sounds as a witness to us centuries later. If you are walking with Christ through your loss, your life is a testimony of faith to others.

Chapter 14

SERVING AT GROUND ZERO

He has put a new song in my mouth—praise to our God;
many will see it and fear, and will trust in the LORD.
Psalm 40:3

Nearly three months after the attacks, Jeanie's first visit to Ground Zero was on a cold December morning; she had come with her teenage son Christopher and several people from her church to serve the firefighters, police officers, and other workers. After taking a ferry from New Jersey to Manhattan, they entered a small church—St. Joseph Chapel on South End Avenue, less than a block from Ground Zero—which had been made into a shelter to provide food and rest for those working in the grueling atmosphere of Ground Zero. Believers were told that the shelter was a place of rest and refuge for the workers—they were asked to keep their voices down, to be respectful and encouraging, and not to talk about personal issues unless the worker initiated it.

Inside the relief center, the atmosphere was quiet—almost reverent. A few computers were lined up on the left for workers to stay in touch with their families through email. There were boxes of donated socks and gloves, useful since the workers had to throw away the heavily soiled ones. On the right were several tables and chairs set up café style. In the back, behind partitions, green military cots with blankets provided a haven for rest.

On the food line, the believers dished up plates of food; they thanked the recovery workers for their hard labor while praying silently for them. With grim, ash-smeared faces, many of the hard-working men and women were obviously exhausted. As believers talked to them, some received prayer or opened up to share about their heavy burdens.

As Jeanie scanned the sooty, somber faces, one young man reminded her of her oldest son, David. She discreetly pointed out the young police officer to Christopher and said, "Doesn't he look just like David?" After the food was served, the believers walked around, offering a ready ear if anyone wanted to talk.

Soon the workers learned that Jeanie had lost her husband Al at Ground Zero. Touched that she would come to serve them, several gathered around her.

"Thank you for coming here," one of them said.

"Oh no, thank you," Jeanie said with fervor. "Thank all of you for the work you're doing for the victims and their families. I'm here to serve you."

The young officer who resembled David took notice of Jeanie's thick Staten Island accent and approached her. They sat down together, and the others moved away. He asked where she was from. It turned out that he also lived on Staten Island with his wife. As they talked, he opened up to Jeanie, telling her how tough it was working at Ground Zero—seeing the dead bodies, knowing that many of his fellow officers had died there, watching mourners come and weep every day. The constant presence of death and tragedy was weighing heavily on him.

"Day in, day out—so much devastation. It's tough," he admitted, his stoic demeanor dropping away as he looked down sadly.

"Yeah, it's tough for me, too," Jeanie said sympathetically. "My husband Al died here."

He looked up at her in surprise; he had not realized this. "And you're here serving us?" he asked. "Why?"

On the tables were scattered several copies of *Calvary Chapel Magazine* which contained an article about Al and his legacy of leading people to Christ on the day of his death. Jeanie opened to the story and handed it to him. "That's my Al," she said. Deeply interested, the man read the entire article.

She added gently, "There's only one thing that's going to get you through this—having a personal relationship with Christ." She told him how Jesus had died on the cross so that he could be forgiven and have eternal life. Romans 10:9 promises *"that if you confess with your mouth the Lord Jesus and believe in your heart that God has raised Him from the dead, you will be saved"* (NKJV). Because Al had done this, she knew he was in heaven with the Lord. "Salvation is a free gift, but you have to accept it by faith. You must repent for your sins and ask God to forgive you."

Jeanie shared how God had comforted her since Al's death and had given her His peace. "Jesus knows what you're going through. He can help you; He can give you His peace." She added, "Would you like to accept Christ?"

He had listened intently, and now he nodded his head 'yes.' Jeanie felt that he would need strong discipleship and support from someone else—preferably a man, someone he could relate to. She called over her pastor, Bruce Koczman of Jesus Fellowship, and another pastor. The young officer and her pastors talked more about salvation, he received a Bible, and then they prayed together.

As Jeanie ministered to other people, she realized that several had heard of Al through the magazines at the center and by word of mouth. After learning that Jeanie had not yet been to the site where Al's building once stood, one of the workers offered to take her and Christopher there in a golf cart. As the cart bumped over the gritty, uneven path, Jeanie prayed silently that God would give her His peace.

It still seemed so surreal. Even though Al's story had been told in several newspapers and magazines, and even though she had shared his legacy with several groups of people, her mind was still trying to comprehend the sobering reality. The pain of Al's death was still fierce.

She sucked in her breath. In front of her loomed a massive gaping chasm covering 16 acres, as if a giant earthquake had opened the ground and sucked the Towers below. All around the hole was a grey concrete retaining wall, with strange rusty spots that had red stains dripping from them—as if they were giant bullet holes made by some horrific weapon. Giant cranes, several stories high, were still lifting enormous steel girders out of the pit. Al's building, all of it, was gone. She had known it was, but seeing it was more of a shock than she had expected.

"It looks like a construction site," 16-year-old Christopher whispered to his mother. Both of them were wearing hard hats for safety.

Here the faces of the workers were even harder—controlled—under the hard hats. Hundreds of men and women bent over their tasks without speaking. Workers in EPA jumpsuits were testing the air that reeked strangely and choked one with invisible dust. No one was laughing or chatting as they worked the heavy equipment on the retaining wall around the site. Some were working frantically, others with a more determined expression.

This isn't about me, is it Lord? Jeanie found herself praying. *You brought me here to minister to these men and women.* As if in answer, she felt the Holy Spirit remind her of a verse she had read:

"Blessed be the God and Father of our Lord Jesus Christ ... who comforts us in all our tribulation, that we may be able to comfort those who are in any trouble, with the comfort with which we ourselves are comforted by God." 2 Corinthians 1:3-4, NKJV

A sense of God's peace filled her heart as she realized He had brought her there to minister to others. The cart stopped, and the driver introduced her to some of his fellow workers, explaining to them that she had lost her husband in 9/11 and that she and Christopher had been serving meals at the center.

They were surprised and grateful. "I just wanted to thank you all for the hard work you're doing for us families. We really appreciate it," Jeanie said. She shared with them how grateful she was that Al's body had been found intact, and that God had helped her through her grief. She told them she knew Al was in heaven because he had accepted Jesus as his personal Savior. They listened with respect. Jeanie felt that God had allowed her to make a connection with them in those few moments. As she finished her four-hour shift, another church group arrived. Through the hours and days, believers gently ministered, praying one-on-one with several people for God's peace, strength, and protection at the center—a special refuge for those sorting through the destruction.

As she made her way home after ministering at Ground Zero, she wished that Al could see how his life and his death for Christ were still touching people's lives. Then she thought—looking up with a smile—maybe he could.

Yea, though I walk through the valley of the shadow of death, I will fear no evil; for You are with me. Psalm 23:4a

She returned to Ground Zero several times to minister to the workers and others who were mourning lost loved ones. Each time, God was present with her—instead of it being a heart-breaking experience, she found herself being a channel of His love to others.

Because she had lost someone in the tragedy, there was an almost instant connection between herself and some of the workers. On her second visit, one of the workers used his torch to make Jeanie a cross out of two torn pieces of steel from Ground Zero; it was about a foot tall. She would treasure it for the rest of her life.

Time after time, rescue workers thanked her for coming, and several people opened up to Jeanie about their own experiences, pain, and questions. "Why had such an awful thing happened? Why would God let so many people die?" As the first young man she had spoken with, many of them were weighed down by the heaviness of death all around them.

She encouraged them to trust in Jesus as Al had done and to have the peace of knowing God and having their sins forgiven. She told all of them that she knew Al was in heaven now because he had accepted Christ as his Savior while on earth. They could have that same assurance. Many listened with respect as she shared the Gospel.

She praised God that Al's desire to share Christ at the World Trade Center was being carried on: through his life and death, through his family's testimony, and through other believers who were ministering in God's name.

Meditation

Blessed be the God and Father of our Lord Jesus Christ ... who comforts us in all our tribulation, that we may be able to comfort those who are in any trouble, with the comfort with which we ourselves are comforted by God.
2 Corinthians 1:3-4, NKJV

After Father God has comforted your heart in a real and personal way, He will bring hurting people into your life for you to comfort. It may be soon, or it may come in time. But He will bring someone in your path that you can comfort as you share the hope and peace you found in Christ. Your words will mean more to that person than those of someone who has not suffered a loss; you have a special authority to speak truth into their lives because of your own suffering. They will listen.

Chapter 15

NO FEAR IN DEATH

And [Stephen] said, "Look! I see the heavens opened
and the Son of Man standing at the right hand of God."
Acts 7:56b

It was a chilly afternoon in December when Amelia and Jeanie were again sitting at Jeanie's kitchen table in deep discussion. Jeanie had been imagining what Al must have gone through between the time the plane hit the building and the towers collapsed. According to reports, it had been roughly an hour and a half.

"It must have been so terrifying for him, trapped in a burning building and knowing he was going to die," Jeanie said, her voice choking with grief. "I can't imagine what he was going through, how he was feeling."

Although her friends and family had tried to shield her from the horrifying details of that day, Jeanie had since come to understand the sequence of events more clearly. After the plane hit the building a few floors below his offices, Al and his coworkers were trapped on the 104th floor. There had been no way out—the elevator was broken, and the stairs were blocked. All they could do was wait as the flames rose higher and higher toward them. Because his body had not burned, Jeanie wondered if Al had simply gone to sleep, asphyxiated by the smoke and fumes. Or was he alive when the building collapsed? Had he felt the crushing weight of the building on top of him? Had he been afraid?

Amelia reached across and took Jeanie's hand. "You don't have to worry about him being terrified," she said gently. "Remember how the Lord was with Stephen?"

Opening her heart to the Lord, Jeanie opened her Bible to Acts Chapter 7. Together, she and Amelia read what Stephen had said right before he was stoned to death by an angry mob of unbelievers.

"But he, being full of the Holy Spirit, gazed into heaven and saw the glory of God, and Jesus standing at the right hand of God, and said, 'Look! I see the heavens opened and the Son of Man standing at the right hand of God.'" Acts 7:56

Amelia pointed out, "Right before he died, he looked up and saw heaven open up. Why would God do that for Stephen and not for Al? I believe He did. I don't believe Al was afraid; I believe he was peaceful because he saw his Lord coming for him."

As she spoke, a deep peace from the Holy Spirit settled over Jeanie's heart, and she knew that Amelia was speaking the truth. Jeanie thanked God for speaking to her again from His Word. He was so personal, so faithful, so kind. How many times had His Word brought the comfort she so desperately needed? And today He had used a dear sister in Christ to speak directly to her fear.

"I'm glad you shared that, Amelia. It's brought me peace," she said. "You're right. I don't think he was terrified."

Jeanie thanked God for being with Al, and for receiving his spirit as He had done with Stephen and so many of His other saints. Maybe Al had even uttered the same words as Stephen when he was dying: "Lord Jesus, receive my spirit." Whatever Al's last words were, she knew God had received his soul into heaven. The Bible is full of promises of eternal life for those who trust in Christ.

"Nevertheless I am continually with you;
You hold me by my right hand.
You will guide me with Your counsel,
And afterward receive me to glory."
Psalm 73:23-24

Just as the Lord had become more real to her, His presence so strong and comforting—she knew He had been with Al. She knew the Lord had guided her beloved husband into the glory of eternity. He had not been alone, as she was not.

Meditation

"Nevertheless I am continually with you;
You hold me by my right hand.
You will guide me with Your counsel,
And afterward receive me to glory."
Psalm 73:23-24

On this journey of grief and perhaps trying to find a 'new normal'
for your life without your loved one, God will walk beside you. He
is continuously with you, whether you feel Him or not. He will hold
your right hand—so close and so personal. If you will let Him, He will
guide you with His counsel, His Word, for the rest of your life. Then,
when your time on earth is also done, He will be there to receive you,
on the other side—the side of glory.

Chapter 16

NEW YEAR'S EVE

Pour out your heart before Him; God is a refuge for us.
Psalm 62:8b

Somehow Jeanie and her family made it through Christmas, and then New Year's Eve 2001 was upon them. They had all gathered at the house of Lorraine and Al Lello, David Braca's in-laws; it was their family tradition to ring in the New Year together. No one had to ask if they would continue the tradition. Everyone knew that this year, more than ever, they all needed to be together.

Jeanie sat surrounded by family—her oldest son David and his wife, Christina, along with her family; Jeanie's daughter Christina and her husband, Greg Cambeis; Jeanie's other daughter Deanna and her husband, Shawn Wirth; Jeanie's son Christopher; and all of the grandchildren. Everyone was there—everyone except Al.

She put a brave face on, trying to enjoy the dinner and games that were part of their family tradition. She remembered when New Year's Eve had been a time of anticipation and excitement—looking ahead to a new year, fresh and promising. But tonight there was no anticipation, no hope of anything new or exciting on the horizon—only a horrible emptiness inside of her. For the hundredth time, Al's absence made her realize how much joy he had brought to their lives. It just didn't feel the same without him; it didn't feel right. Several times that evening, she felt tears rising to her throat, but she willed herself not to cry in front of the family. She knew they were all doing their best to go on without Al, and she would not distress them further with her tears.

At midnight, everyone hugged and kissed; soon after, they dispersed to go home and put children to bed. Christopher went with one of his siblings while Jeanie got into her car alone. As soon as she shut the door, under the cover of darkness, tears began to pour from her eyes. A wordless sob rose from her throat, and the immense pain that she had been suppressing all evening began to rush to the surface and break forth, like mighty waves rising from the sea. Again and again the sobs came; her tears would not stop falling. "Oh Al," she whispered.

She turned the key and started to drive. Without really thinking about it, she was heading toward Fairview Cemetery in Middletown, NJ, where Al had been buried less than three months ago.

She noted with relief that hers was the only car in the cemetery. Not bothering with an umbrella, she got out in the rainy night and walked to Al's grave. Her aching heart was racing; she couldn't move fast enough. When she got to his grave, she crumpled to her knees, head bent, tears mingling with rain and falling to the sacred ground.

For a few minutes she just sobbed; then the sobs turned into wails. She barely felt the trembling of her body in the chilling rain, so hot was her heart burning in her chest. Then words began to pour out between the sobs, "Oh Al, it's so hard. I don't know if I can really do this—what God has called me to do—to go on without you here. I don't know if I can make it." It seemed that all the fear and sorrow that had been building inside her for the past three months had been set loose.

In the darkness and inner turmoil, she knew she was still in God's presence, and her emotions and fears rose up in a wordless prayer. Thoughts began to race through her mind: *How am I going to make it without Al? Will it always hurt so much? I'm a widow now; what does that mean, Lord? How am I supposed to function in that role? Was it okay to grieve like this, to mourn? How often?* For the past three months, the pain had been present—every day, some worse than others. She hurt all the time, but she knew that she was supposed to go on with her life. Even now, in the midst of her heart breaking, she still wanted to give God glory. She just didn't know how.

Then she felt the presence of the Lord—gentle, understanding, comforting. She knew He was right there with her and that He understood her pain. She also sensed that He was mourning with her, as Jesus had done with Mary the day he came to raise Lazarus from the dead.

As she learned to do long ago, she reached out to God from the depths of her heart. "Oh God help me," she whispered. "Help all of us—all the wives and children and families—tonight. It's our first New Year's Eve without our loved ones." Again, she felt God's comfort and peace; she knew He had heard her prayers. She also felt His compassion, letting her know that it was all right to cry or yell or whatever she needed to do. She could do it alone with Him; she could pour out her pain to Him.

She sensed Him urging her to stay close to Him—not to harden her heart or withdraw from His presence. She also sensed that He loved her no matter what, and that He understood—better than anyone could—what she was going through.

She sat in the cold, shaking and shivering as rain poured from the black sky. She wanted to stay there forever; she didn't want to go home to her empty house. As if frozen in place, she stayed kneeling in the dark for about 20 minutes. The rain continued to wet her face, but her tears began to slow.

Finally, Jeanie realized that her body was chilled and needed to get warm again. Reluctantly she got to her feet, numb and spent. She felt the Lord's presence go with her as she got back in her car and drove home.

As she walked into the quiet house, her swollen eyes were dry and her heart was numb. Mechanically she got ready for bed and lay her head on the pillow. Still she felt God's presence with her, and wordlessly thanked Him for not leaving her alone. She knew He would be there when she woke up. She knew He would be with her in the new year ahead.

Meditation

Pour out your heart before Him;
God is a refuge for us.
Psalm 62:8b

There are times to weep. Times to get alone with God and just pour out our grief. Reach out to Him in those moments, and you will find that He is a refuge for you there.

Chapter 17

BLESSINGS AT BIBLE STUDY

*Though the fig tree may not blossom, nor fruit be on the vines
... yet I will rejoice in the LORD, I will joy in the God of my salvation.*
Habakkuk 3:17-18

The day after New Year's Day was a Wednesday. And every Wednesday, several of her sisters in Christ would gather at Jeanie's house for their weekly Bible study. After September 11, Jeanie had felt that she should continue to host the study and enjoy fellowship with other believers. Peggy Cuozzo, whose husband Gary was the assistant pastor at Calvary Chapel Four Winds at the time, led the study and taught the women directly from the word.

Having their weekly fellowship had meant more to Jeanie than she could have imagined. Not only did it break the silence and sobriety of her quiet home, but it lifted her spirits and fed her soul. Every week she was strengthened and encouraged as ladies of various ages gathered around her living room with Bibles on their laps, laughing, talking, and crying together. They shared their struggles openly and prayed specifically for each other. It was a blessing for Jeanie in many ways: the fellowship, the accountability, the presence of other close believers on a regular basis. But most of all, she was strengthened by the Word.

They were studying through the Book of Habakkuk. Jeanie had learned that the name Habakkuk means "embracer" or "embrace." She reflected that the word had special meaning for her now since she had decided to embrace, or accept, her loss as being from the Lord. She was learning to embrace God's will for her, whatever He wanted to do—both in her own heart and through her life—to glorify Himself. She also realized that she had felt God's embrace—His intimate closeness, His love, His heartbeat—during her time of sorrow and loneliness as never before.

As part of the study, the women were to read through each chapter on their own. God began to speak to Jeanie about her situation directly through the Old Testament book that had been written more than 2,500 years ago. She read, *"But the LORD is in His holy temple. Let all the earth keep silence before Him"* (Hab. 2:20). She felt the Holy Spirit speaking to her heart: Even though at times she wanted to cry, argue with God, or fight back because of what had happened, she was to abide before the Lord in quiet reverence.

She felt she understood what He was saying. Many people had been angered by the attack on the towers; there were arguments and protests about fighting the terrorists or getting revenge. But when she read those words, it was almost as if He said audibly, "Jeanie, I don't want you to be a part of that. I have a different way that I want you to go. I have a message for you to share."

Again she acknowledged, "Yes, Lord, I hear You. Whatever You want for me, I'll do it."

Soon after, she was reading Chapter 3, in which the prophet Habakkuk declared that no matter what happened in his life—whether seasons of plenty or of barrenness—he would always praise God. Jeanie stopped at this passage and read it several times, her eyes filling with tears:

> *Though the fig tree may not blossom,*
> *Nor fruit be on the vines;*
> *Though the labor of the olive may fail,*
> *And the fields yield no food;*
> *Though the flock may be cut off from the fold,*
> *And there be no herd in the stalls—*
>
> *Yet I will rejoice in the LORD,*
> *I will joy in the God of my salvation.*
> *The LORD God is my strength;*
> *He will make my feet like deer's feet,*
> *And He will make me walk on my high hills.*
> Habbakuk 3:17-19a

Alone in her room with her Bible open, she acknowledged out loud what God was speaking to her heart. "Yes, Lord. I will rejoice in You. No matter what—though You took Al away, though You take my health away. I will praise You. You are the God of my salvation," she declared the words before God with fervent conviction.

As she re-read part of verse 19, she smiled: *"The Lord God is my strength."* Yes, He was becoming her strength. Now that other things she had depended on had been taken away, she had only God to lean on. And in leaning on Him, she had discovered how close He truly was—how faithful, how personal, how real.

She continued to read, *"He will make my feet like deer's feet."* She realized He had allowed her to go to many places she would never have gone before; she was actually standing before crowds of people boldly sharing her faith on a regular basis. And because of her situation, people were listening. God was using it for His glory.

Further, she read, *"and He will make me walk on my high hills."* She felt this was a promise from the Lord that there would also be joy in the midst of her pain—that He would give her seasons of tremendous blessing and closeness with Him. He would raise her to new heights in her faith; she would taste of His joy and peace in a special way.

A few weeks later, she came across Psalm 119:50, which says, *"This is my comfort in my affliction, for Your word has given me life."* She had always read her Bible on a regular basis, but after 9/11 it had become her lifeline. Her constant comfort through all of the grieving and confusion had been God's Word. It had given her hope in the darkest of times. She realized that God was using His Word to literally give her life—to strengthen her emotionally and spiritually so that she could go on day after day. *I feel like His Word is breathing life back into my soul,* she thought. Every private time she spent alone with the Lord was a healing time.

His Word also guided her. She also saw that, whether she realized it or not in the moment, God was showing her the way to go in every situation. He was protecting her and speaking to her through His Word.

Her true hope was not in the future or external things or people or even herself; it was in His Word. She clung to His promises that He had made her—that He loved her, that He would never forsake her.

So many times she had recited these promises aloud to herself as the Holy Spirit brought them to her remembrance. In times of loneliness, she had found great comfort in Jesus' words, *"I am with you always, even to the end of the age"* (Matthew 28:20b), or the Lord's tender declaration, "Yes, I have loved you with an everlasting love; therefore with lovingkindness I have drawn you" (Jeremiah 31:3).

And she knew God's Word better now than ever—partly because she was sharing it as never before. Knowing that she would be going before a crowd of people to speak from the Word made her study it more diligently. The more she took in, the more she had to give others. And, amazingly, the more she devoured God's Word, the more it strengthened her soul. *This is how I'm going to make it,* she realized one night. *By staying in the Word.*

Meditation

Though the fig tree may not blossom, nor fruit be on the vines ... yet I will rejoice in the LORD, I will joy in the God of my salvation.
Habakkuk 3:17-18

When times of sadness, hardship, leanness, or emptiness come into our lives, we have a unique opportunity. We can choose to rejoice in the One who will never change, the One who will never fail. We can even take joy in the God of our salvation—simply because He loves us and has saved us. If all God ever did for us was save us and give us a place in heaven, that alone would be enough to praise Him forever. But He gives us so much more. Let us rejoice in Him, even when the checking account is empty or the house is quiet. He Himself is with us. He will bring us through these times.

Chapter 18

A GOOD CRY

To everything there is a season,
A time for every purpose under heaven:
A time to weep, And a time to laugh;
A time to mourn, And a time to dance.
Ecclesiastes 3:1, 4

Bear one another's burdens, and so fulfill the law of Christ.
Galatians 6:2

In January, Jeanie's youngest son was heavy on her heart. It was just herself and Christopher at home now. Although each of them had spoken publicly before crowds about Al's death, they still had not discussed it privately. Jeanie had wanted to give her son the space he needed, and she prayed for God to open a door to talk when he was ready.

In his sophomore year of high school, he had been coming home from school later and later. She knew he hung out with his friends a lot and was heavily involved in the drama program. He loved singing and acting, and was quite good at it. But she wondered whether he was uncomfortable in their new home or if he didn't like coming home. They had moved in less than a month before 9/11, and she had done her best to make it feel like home. But she knew that it probably felt strange—not like home at all—without his dad there.

In the spring of 2002, one night after Jeanie had eaten dinner alone again, God opened that door. Christopher came home and went into his room without saying much. Before 9/11, he had always been happy and chatty—a bit of an entertainer and an extrovert. Asking the Lord for wisdom, she knocked on his door.

"Yeah?" came his mumbled reply through the closed door.

She cracked open the door and smiled at him. "Hi honey, can I come in?" He didn't meet her gaze but nodded.

She sat on the edge of the bed beside him. "What's the matter—don't you want to eat here anymore?" she asked. He shrugged.

"Are you all right?" she asked gently. "Do you want to talk?" Jeanie waited. She did not break the silence that followed, letting Christopher search his own heart and sort through his feelings.

After a few minutes, Christopher said, "I miss him."

"I miss him, too. I understand how you feel," she said.

Christopher began talking about his dad—how Al had always made him laugh, how he always knew the right answers, how he had always told Christopher that he loved him. He remembered how, whenever he had needed time with his dad, Al would always stop what he was doing and listen to his youngest son. Then Christopher's voice choked, and he stopped talking.

"Please, Christopher, if you need to cry, let it out. Don't hold it in," she said.

The tears began falling, and soon he was sobbing in Jeanie's arms. She began to cry too. She felt the Lord's presence with them as they were able to let their grief out together after so many months of holding back. After several minutes, Christopher said frankly, "This sucks!"

Jeanie laughed in the midst of her crying. He sat up beside her, and soon they were both laughing in relief and wiping their eyes.

"Thanks, mom. I feel like—like a huge weight has been lifted off me. Like I can finally breathe," he said. They talked for a while longer, their old camaraderie returning. The wall of silence between them had been broken.

"Do you know what I hate?" he said, rolling his eyes.

"What?" she said, smiling. It was good to see his old eye-rolling expression. She had missed his animated conversation.

"When people come up to me and say, 'How are you?' and I say, 'Fine.' And then they give me this look and say, 'How are you, *really*?' I hate that question," he said.

Jeanie nodded. She knew it was good for Christopher to talk out his feelings with her, here in the safety of their home where he could cry or laugh and just be himself. She thanked God for opening the communication between them.

A few days later, he came home and called out, "Hey mom, how are you?"

"I'm fine honey," she said, turning to look at him.

"No—how are you *really*?" he said, wiggling his eyebrows at her. They both laughed. That question would become a running joke between them—a way of coping with their loss and staying connected. Jeanie smiled. It was just like something Al would have done—using humor to lighten a hard situation. He always used to crack jokes with her and the kids. As she laughed at Christopher and hugged him, she was thankful that he was so much like his father. She was also glad that God had lifted some of the heaviness that had been in their home for the past few months.

It was a fulfillment of the prophetic Scripture that Isaiah wrote about Christ: *"The Spirit of the Lord GOD is upon Me, Because the LORD has anointed Me ... to console those who mourn in Zion, to give them beauty for ashes, the oil of joy for mourning, the garment of praise for the spirit of heaviness"* (Isaiah 61:1, 3). God had given them joy again.

Meditation

*The Spirit of the Lord GOD is upon Me
... to console those who mourn in Zion,
to give them beauty for ashes ... joy for mourning
... praise for the spirit of heaviness*
Isaiah 61: 1a, 3b

Do you need the Lord to restore your joy? That's one of the things He can do in our lives. Ask Him to give you joy, to fill you with His Holy Spirit and lift the heaviness from your heart. Even after devastating loss and grief, Christ can anoint us with new joy. It may take time, but joy will come.

Chapter 19

A REFUGE IN THE STORM

In the shadow of Your wings I will make my refuge,
until these calamities have passed by.
Psalm 57:1b

By the spring of 2002, Jeanie had grown to dread leaving her house. It seemed everywhere she turned, there were photos of the smoking Twin Towers or the gruesome devastation of Ground Zero. The worst were the pictures of Al's building on fire; she had to force herself not to think of him trapped inside as the room got hotter and filled with smoke. She knew that he had died with the peace of God, but seeing his building on fire pierced her heart deeply. She avoided listening to the news reports or getting enmeshed in the politics of the situation; for her, it was too personal. Her most important priorities were staying close to the Lord as He continued to heal her, and being there for her family.

She was still worried about Christopher. While he maintained his high GPA and his standing in the National Honor Society, he was so busy that she rarely saw him. True, he was heavily involved with theater and extracurricular activities at school, but she still wondered if he dreaded coming home. She couldn't blame him, she thought, looking at their kitchen table piled with papers from the U.S. government and the American Red Cross—more paperwork sent every week for family members of the 9/11 victims. Then there were the phone calls every day—sometimes reporters, sometimes friends or family members. Time and again, she had to repeat things that she would rather forget. Sometimes she was glad he wasn't there to hear her recount the horrible events or her feelings about the past six months. Life was a strange, swirling blur, and Jeanie felt like she was starting to drown in it all.

One day in February she was on the phone with Peggy and Gary Cuozzo. "It's everywhere—everywhere I turn, everywhere I go—pictures of it, people talking about it. I can't escape. And I know it's not easy on Christopher either. We can't go through one day in peace," she said.

The Cuozzos were at their winter home in southern Florida, and Gary offered, "Jeanie, why don't you two come down and stay with us? You love the beach and the warmer weather."

Peggy chimed in, "It will do you good, Jeanie."

Jeanie called Christopher's principal, Dan Lane. She remembered seeing him at a parents' night only two weeks after 9/11. He had seemed compassionate and understanding about what she and Christopher were going through. On the phone with Principal Lane, she asked if she could take Christopher to Florida for a time of rest and healing. "We need to get out of this town. Could he please come with me?" Jeanie asked.

"Absolutely," he said.

"I don't want him to have to worry about homework and classes. Can you support me in this?" Jeanie asked. He agreed.

The invitation was extended to include Al's 70-year-old Aunt Anna. Jeanie knew Al had shared the Gospel with her several times, and she wondered if God had a special purpose for Anna's coming.

A few days later, the three of them were on a plane to southwest Florida. Jeanie and Christopher didn't say much; they were both looking forward to solitude and quiet—away from newspapers, TV reports, people calling with questions. A place where they could work through their grief or let their minds think of other things. Jeanie was also hoping for a visit to Calvary Chapel Fort Lauderdale. Peggy had given her some Bible-teaching tapes from there.

After being greeted by warm embraces from the Cuozzos, the trio of Jeanie, Christopher, and Aunt Anna settled in to the comfortable townhouse. Christopher spent a lot of time sitting on the deck looking at the sea. Jeanie went for quiet strolls by the water.

Walking on the beach with its turquoise waves and fine white sand, Jeanie remembered walking on a similar beach with Al nearly eight months ago. When they purchased their new home in 2001, there were a few things at the house which needed to be worked on. So she and Al had gone away for a week in the Bahamas in early August. She realized now that it had been a gift from the Lord, a last romantic retreat for the two of them. She began to see how kind the Lord had been in giving them that time together. He even allowed Al to give away their daughter Deanna in marriage less than two months before he died.

She remembered Deanna's wedding. It had been a beautiful sunny day in July. That morning, as she and Al and Deanna had driven to the church in a limousine, Al had smiled proudly at Deanna and said, "I love you." She had hugged him and said, "I love you too, Dad." Everything had been perfect, like a dream. They had pulled up to Tower Hill Presbyterian Church—a traditional, picturesque white church with a stately steeple and ornate stained glass windows that was perched on a hill.

Al had walked Deanna down the aisle in front of more than 200 people. She had looked so beautiful with her dark hair pulled up and her gauzy white veil framing her delicate Italian features. Al had been so caught up in the moment that as soon as they got to the altar, he pulled up her veil and kissed her—something he was supposed to do a few minutes later. Deanna had giggled. Jeanie smiled now at the memory. Then the minister had asked who gave her away, and Al had said, "My wife and I," and had kissed his daughter again. That was July 21—seven weeks before Al had died. Two months later they had his memorial service at the same church. It still seemed so surreal.

The solitude allowed her to reminisce about her family, to recall those moments with Al and her family and to savor them in her heart. Immersing herself in such happy memories helped to ease the pain.

A few days later, Jeanie went with Peggy to the women's Bible study at her Baptist church in Naples. Jeanie was asked to share with the whole group.

That Tuesday morning she stood before several hundred women at First Baptist Church Naples. The ladies listened attentively as Jeanie related her experience and how she had discovered that Al had been leading a group of coworkers in prayer before they all perished. The women were so touched that the pastor's wife, Janet Wicker, called and asked if Jeanie could share with another ladies' group on Wednesday night.

"I'm sorry, Janet," Jeanie heard Peggy say into the phone. "Jeanie has been wanting to visit a church in Fort Lauderdale, and that's what we have planned for Wednesday."

Even though it was a two-hour drive to Calvary Chapel Fort Lauderdale, Aunt Anna readily agreed to join them. Their small party sat on the second row—a difficult spot to secure in the megachurch. During the message, Aunt Anna listened intently. Jeanie knew that Al had shared God's Word with her several times. Although Aunt Anna had a fear and respect for God, she did not have a personal relationship with Jesus Christ. When the speaker gave an invitation for people to accept Jesus Christ as their Savior, the elderly woman jumped out of her chair and grabbed Christopher's hand, saying, "Come with me." The two of them went forward together. Jeanie was overjoyed. *Thank You, Lord. You knew this was where she needed to be tonight, that she was ready to accept You.*

The next morning at breakfast, they all bowed their heads to thank the Lord for their food—a custom that the Bracas always followed. Aunt Anna interjected, "I'd like to pray." Jeanie and Christopher looked at her with pleasant surprise. "I have never prayed out loud before in my entire life, but I'd like to pray today," she said. Smiling, they all bowed their heads as Aunt Anna addressed her Savior—this time, as His daughter. Jeanie's eyes filled with happy tears. *Al, can you see this?* she thought. She could almost feel him rejoicing with her.

Meditation

In the shadow of Your wings I will make my refuge,
until these calamities have passed by.
Psalm 57:1b

Sometimes we need to get away with the Lord—away from our familiar surroundings, or places that stir painful memories. Ask the Lord to bring you to a place where you can be with Him in peace and quiet. It may be a beach retreat, mountain getaway, or just a nearby park. It is helpful to go and get away with Him. Let His peace fill you and restore your soul.

He leads me beside the still waters;
He restores my soul.
Psalm 23:2b, 3a

Chapter 20

A TIME TO SPEAK

A time to keep silence, and a time to speak.
Eccesiastes 3:7b

Knowing that it was important to share Al's testimony and the Gospel, Jeanie and Christopher continued to speak in a variety of venues whenever a door opened—sometimes separately, sometimes together. Many doors opened to speak in 2002. Young Christopher addressed several thousand people at the PNC Bank Arts Center in Holmdel, NJ, at a memorial service. He told the massive crowd: "He was a great father. He never set restrictions, but taught us right from wrong by using the Bible. He taught me how to love and how to be a man of God."

In August of 2002, Chris was one of five teenagers to share on a CBS television show about 9/11. Both Jeanie and Chris were featured in multiple newspapers and magazines.

Also in 2002, the two of them even agreed to let a Japanese film crew come in to their home to make a documentary. They felt it would be an opportunity to be a witness to people in another country about having a personal relationship with Jesus Christ.

But after a year and a half in the spotlight, the constant interviews and pressure began to wear on both of them.

One day Christopher announced, "Mom, I'm not going to do this anymore."

Jeanie knew that he was specifically referring to the film crew that had followed them around in their home for nearly two months, even taping the women's Bible study. Now that the taping was over, she felt that she should not allow another camera crew in their home. It had been too hard—for both of them. They had been unable to work through their grief with cameras always on them.

"Yeah, I don't want to do that again," she agreed. And they didn't. But they prayed that, somewhere in Japan, someone had been touched by seeing the lives of believers who were mourning the loss of their husband and father while continuing to walk with Jesus Christ.

Meditation

A time to keep silence, and a time to speak.
Ecclessiastes 3:7b

While the Lord may open doors for you to speak about your loved one or to share the Gospel, other times He may also lead you to rest and quiet. Be sensitive to His leading. It is OK to say 'no' sometimes if you feel you're not ready or the time is not right for you to pour out for others.

Chapter 21

CLEANING OUT THE CLOSET

For I, the LORD your God, will hold your right hand, saying to you,
"Fear not, I will help you."
Isaiah 41:13

The Lord brought Jeanie closure in varying degrees, sometimes through practical things. In March of 2002, nearly six months after 9/11, Jeanie was confronted with the fact that the walk-in closet in their bedroom needed repairs. There was just one problem—she would have to remove Al's things. She had put it off for months. She dreaded it, remembering how hard it had been to remove his shaver and soap from the shower: Somehow that little act had made his absence more real, more permanent. It said, "He's not coming back—ever."

It wasn't just a closet. There were memories and emotions hanging inside. When she looked at his suits and shirts, it felt like he was still living there—just away on a business trip. His clothes were one of her last, remaining connections to Al.

She fancied that some of them still smelled like him. Smells were very powerful for Jeanie; she kept his cologne on her dresser—something she would continue to do for the next decade. She would close her eyes, inhale the familiar fragrance, and be transported back to special times they had shared together—romantic dinners out, Al holding her close under the stars, dancing together at their children's weddings.

That week, Amelia came over to do the ironing, and Jeanie confessed her problem. She knew she needed to clean out and repair the closet, but couldn't face it alone. The two set a date to tackle it together.

The morning came. With a shaky determination, Jeanie led Amelia and a friend named Barbara into the bedroom to sort through Al's things. They decided to make piles of what was to be kept or given to charity. As Jeanie clutched two of Al's suits and carried them out of the closet, her knees grew weak. She had to sit down suddenly on the white chair. Her fingers ran over the material of Al's clothes. *He wore these. They touched him. They belonged to him. He always looked so smart in his suits going to work every day.* The physical touch of his clothing reminded her so strongly of him that her heart was pierced with a deep ache. She missed his physical presence. She wanted to hug the suits, to hug Al again. She started crying quietly. Amelia and Barbara noticed her sitting down and came over.

"I can't do this," Jeanie sobbed. "I'm sorry. This is too hard. I—I can't even stand up."

"We'll do it, Jeanie," Amelia said gently. "You just sit there and tell us what to do."

All day they worked as Jeanie directed them to keep things, throw them away, or give them to charity. She tested her strength a few times and still felt that if she tried to stand, she would pass out. So she sat for hours in the chair, watching as one after another of Al's things were brought out, set before her, and then taken away. It was grueling.

Jeanie felt empty. As his belongings were sorted into piles, it felt surreal—almost as if she was an observer watching a movie. Her heart would not stop aching, and her mind kept repeating, *It wasn't supposed to end this way. We were supposed to go to Hawaii. We were supposed to enjoy life together after he retired. We were supposed to grow old together.*

At the end of the day, after Amelia and Barbara had gone and taken away some of Al's belongings, Jeanie sat quietly again in her white armchair. The closet looked so empty. Too empty.

Logically, she knew it had to be cleared out for the repairman, but it looked worse than just an empty closet—it looked desolate. There was just a big, dark hole where all of his things had been. It looked like she felt—like something was missing, like there was a gaping hole inside. Exhausted from head to toe, she turned away and got ready for bed.

Deep in her heart, in the place where she had been hearing God's voice so often, she felt as if the reality of her widowhood was settling in. It was almost as if God was saying, *That season is over. It's time to accept that your former life—your married life with Al—is over. Things will be different from now on. But stay close to Me.*

She felt numb, but yielded to the new reality. She knew she must accept this new level of letting go. It was her Savior's will. Tucking herself into her empty bed, she pulled out her Bible and read the Psalms.

I know, LORD, that your laws are righteous,
and that in faithfulness you have afflicted me.
May your unfailing love be my comfort,
according to your promise to your servant.
Let your compassion come to me that I may live,
for your law is my delight.
Psalm 119:75-77, NIV

Reading the words with an open heart, she felt the comfort of God's presence. As she turned out the light and lay wearily down on her pillow, two things were very clear: Her life with Al on this earth was over; things would never be the same. But she also knew that Jesus was still with her.

Meditation

For I, the LORD your God, will hold your right hand,
saying to you, "Fear not, I will help you."
Isaiah 41:13

The grieving process is just that—a process. The Lord in His gentleness may allow you to walk through it one layer at a time. As new emotions or experiences come up that cause you sadness or in which you have to choose again to let go of your loved one, know that God is with you and He will help you. There is no condemnation in grieving. God understands your heart and your emotions, even if you do not. He doesn't condemn our tears; He holds us close.

Chapter 22

WIDOWHOOD: A NEW CALLING

For the Lord your God is God of gods and Lord of lords,
the great God, mighty and awesome.
...He defends the cause of the fatherless and the widow.
Deuteronomy 10:17-18a, NIV

As was still her custom, Jeanie sat in her white armchair with her Bible one morning in late March of 2002. She had come to seek the Lord. Even though it had only been about six months, it seemed like an eternity since that beautiful morning on 9/11. She remembered sitting in that same chair and feeling Him speak so clearly to her, preparing her for what lay ahead. Since that moment, life had been a blur—planning the memorial service, enduring the constant mountains of paperwork, speaking in front of large groups of people, even making the small innumerable changes in her everyday routines.

But this morning she had something deeper on her mind that she wanted to talk over with her Heavenly Father. Something that only He could answer. She was ready to face the reality that she could no longer call herself Al's wife; she was a widow.

Widow. She let that word echo in her mind. She said it aloud, "I'm a widow." She felt a blankness, an emptiness. The word seemed strange on her tongue, like a foreign word. Then she turned her thoughts to God.

"Father, how do I do this? How do I live as a widow? How do I act, think, function as a widow?" she asked honestly, wanting an answer.

She realized that she had identified herself so long as Al's wife that it felt odd to see herself in any other way. And she couldn't throw herself into the familiar role of motherhood because all of her children were grown; even her youngest, Christopher, was becoming a young man and was hardly ever home.

So here she was—just Jeanie. If she wasn't married, was she single now? She couldn't even remember what it had been like to be single in her early 20s. She didn't feel single: So much of her heart still felt joined to Al.

Sure, she had learned many practical things that had helped her to adjust to her new role. Mary Jane had taken her to the bank to open a checking account. Gary Cuozzo had introduced her to financial advisors. She had never even written a check before 9/11; Al had always just left some cash for her on the dresser every morning. With a bond trader for a husband, she had been happy to let him handle all of the finances. Thankfully, he had kept excellent records, and their finances were in good shape. Jeanie knew she was the head of their home now and was trying to be a good steward, to do things the way Al would have done them.

But those were just surface things. Today she wanted to talk to the Lord about her identity. *Who am I now?* she thought.

She had mentioned her perplexity to Candice Beckelman, her pastor's wife, not too long ago.

"Candice, I just don't know where I fit in here anymore," she had confessed privately.

Candice, who had been at their church for less than a year, said with a smile, "Neither do I, Jeanie. Let's seek the Lord together." The two of them had started meeting once a week to seek the Lord and pray together.

This morning, as she pondered her new identity, Jeanie felt the Holy Spirit prompting her to seek the truth in God's Word. She remembered Paul's encouragement in 2 Timothy 3:16 that said, "All Scripture is given by inspiration of God, and is profitable for doctrine, for reproof, for correction, for instruction in righteousness." If she needed to know what to do in a situation, she could look to the Word. That's where she always found answers for every need, every problem, every situation. The Scriptures had been her constant comfort, her source of inspiration, hope, and instruction through these dark and confusing months.

So today she would seek God's truth about her new identity, her new lifestyle. She turned to her concordance to look up as many verses as she could find that contained the word "widow."

She read in Deuteronomy 10 that God "administers justice for the fatherless and the widow." That gave her comfort—to know that God would take care of her and Christopher, and see that they were treated fairly. She knew that vulnerable people were often targets. She realized that He already had taken care of her—by sending close trusted friends to advise her, to teach her about money. Then she found several verses in Deuteronomy 24 in which God provided food for the fatherless and widow; she knew He would provide all of their needs. Without Al to take care of these practical things, they could trust in God to. Mentally entrusting their needs to God, Jeanie found herself feeling more peaceful.

Then she came to the story of a woman named Anna in Luke Chapter 2 and read it with great interest. Mary and Joseph had brought the baby Jesus to the temple in Jerusalem to dedicate Him to the Lord. The prophet Simeon had blessed him, prophesying that He would bring salvation to Jews and Gentiles. The only other person to recognize Him as Messiah was Anna, an 84-year-old widow. Jeanie eagerly devoured the description of this Hebrew woman:

> *Now there was one, Anna, a prophetess, the daughter of Phanuel, of the tribe of Asher. She was of a great age, and had lived with a husband seven years from her virginity; and this woman was a widow of about eighty-four years, who did not depart from the temple, but served God with fastings and prayers night and day. And coming in that instant she gave thanks to the Lord, and spoke of Him to all those who looked for redemption in Jerusalem.*
> Luke 2:36-38

Jeanie was intrigued by this description of Anna. She had been a prophetess, a special messenger from God to speak His words to the people. She had been widowed for decades. She had been married a shorter time than Jeanie—only seven years—and she had never remarried. Jeanie noted that Anna "did not depart from the temple"—she stayed close to God's house and God's people. And she "served God with fastings and prayers night and day." She was a woman of prayer, ready to intercede day and night. And after she encountered Jesus, she spoke about Him all over Jerusalem.

Suddenly Jeanie had a new vision for her life. She prayed, "Oh Lord, make me like Anna. Let me stay close to Your house and Your people. I know that there I can serve You, and there I will be safe. That's where I belong. And make me a woman of prayer, to really intercede for people, to fast for others. I know with my diabetes that I can't fast very much, but give me strength and wisdom to do it when You want me to. And Lord, I want to tell others what You have done for me—to tell them about their Savior."

She felt a new clarity: God still had things for her to do—a reason for keeping her here on earth. She would be a woman who served God, who prayed, and who pointed others to the Messiah, Jesus Christ. "Yes, Father, make me like Anna." She would go to the prayer meeting at church every Monday, and she would continue to be a facilitator for a women's Bible study at the church on Wednesday nights.

Shortly thereafter, she was reading Luke 2:49, in which the boy Jesus tells Mary and Joseph, *"Why did you seek Me? Did you not know that I must be about My Father's business?"*

She meditated on those Words, put the Bible down, and prayed, "Father, please allow me to go about Your business every day. Put someone in front of me everywhere I go. Show me the way to go. I still want to minister to others and be a witness for You." She knew that it was no longer her place to minister to couples at church, which she had done for years alongside her husband. She asked silently, *Lord, how should I serve You?*

She felt the Lord urging her to minister to others from her own experiences. She was to comfort others as she herself had received comfort by the Lord. But she must be willing and open to His leading.

A familiar verse came to her mind: *"Blessed be the God and Father of our Lord Jesus Christ, the Father of mercies and God of all comfort, who comforts us in all our tribulation, that we may be able to comfort those who are in any trouble, with the comfort with which we ourselves are comforted by God."* 2 Corinthians 1:3-4

She felt Him clearly tell her that she had a choice: She could dwell on her own heartache, or she could love others and let God use her life in a special way. So in her heart, she surrendered again to the Lord. "Yes, Lord, use me. Use my life."

Over the next few weeks, God began to open doors. As she went about her daily activities—going to the grocery store, running errands—she always wore a smile and tried to show the love of Christ. She was ready to listen to people and to share about Jesus. And she found that God often brought into her path those who were hurting—a waitress, a lady in the check-out line, even a woman standing on the street corner crying for her deceased child. She called these "divine appointments"—encounters that had obviously been orchestrated by the hand of God. She began to get out of bed every morning with an expectation that God would use her.

When Jeanie would talk to people, she tried to look below the surface. She listened with sensitivity, asking the Holy Spirit to give her discernment or a special word of encouragement for them. Many times she shared her own pain—genuinely, often with tears—as she talked about how the Lord was her Comforter, her Keeper, and her Savior. It became a lifelong practice for her, to be ready to share the Gospel wherever she went—to see every person as important enough to take the time to listen—as Jesus had done. She was keenly aware that everyone's time on earth is short.

Having experienced such deep pain, she also had a new compassion. And when someone she knew was going through a loss or some other grief, she would gently ask, "How are you doing?" She would listen attentively, letting the Lord open a deeper conversation about their spiritual or emotional well-being. She eagerly encouraged people to stay close to God and regularly read His Word. Then she would pray for them—both while she was with them and often after she left. As she prayed, if the Lord brought a person back to her mind, she called them on the phone to check on them. People seemed touched that she remembered them and their problems, and that she would go to the trouble to call them.

Jeanie's life became one of reaching out, of ministering to others, of being a walking witness for Jesus Christ. She began to realize that being a widow was not a curse or a punishment; it was part of her new calling from God.

Since 9/11, she had received hundreds of cards and letters from people all over the world, and she had responded to each one. Those letters had been such a blessing to her that she realized she could also use words to build others up. She began a new ministry of encouragement through letters and cards—if anyone was sick, or celebrating an anniversary, or if people needed encouragement—she would write to them. She would pray over each card, and let the person know that they were in her prayers. She could do this whether she was confined to bed or not feeling well; her ministry of encouragement could continue on.

Meditation

"Why did you seek Me? Did you not know that I must be about My Father's business?" Luke 2:49

Even after loss, the Father still has a plan for your life. Seek Him; ask Him what He would have you do. Start each day with an expectation that God has a plan for this day; set your mind to be about your Father's business. Your life is not over; He still has plans for you.

Chapter 23

TESTIFYING OF GOD'S FAITHFULNESS

The Lord GOD has given Me the tongue of the learned,
that I should know how to speak a word in season to him who is weary.
He awakens Me morning by morning, He awakens My ear
to hear as the learned. The Lord GOD has opened My ear;
and I was not rebellious, nor did I turn away. Isaiah 50:4-5

In spring 2002, Jeanie had run into Sandy MacIntosh and Cheryl Brodersen at the East Coast Pastors' Wives Conference in Sandy Cove, Maryland. Cheryl relayed a message from her husband, Pastor Brian, that Jeanie should write a book about Al's testimony and what God had been doing in her life since 9/11. Jeanie was stunned. But, as she had been learning over the past year, she kept her heart open to whatever the Lord wanted her to do.

Today, she called Pastor Jim for her regular dose of encouragement and perspective. She related that, though she was still working through her grief, she was trying to see the bigger picture.

"I know God is in charge, and that He has a plan in all of this," she told him with quiet confidence. "I know that all things work together for good for those who love God, like it says in Romans 8:28. I know He is my strength, and that He is going to get me through all of this, every day."

She added, "I want this all to be used for His glory. I want His will, that it would somehow bless others." Jim agreed that her desire was a good one and offered encouragement through Scripture. As was their custom, they prayed and hung up the phone.

Less than half an hour later, Jeanie's phone rang again. This time it was Jim's wife, Mary Ann.

"Jeanie, would you be willing to share what has happened in your life and minister to the ladies at our church?" Mary Ann asked. "We have a spring brunch planned for the ladies, and I was praying for a speaker."

Jeanie's heart leaped. Perhaps this was part of God's plan! Perhaps He could use all of this loss and devastation—and the comfort He had given her in the midst of it—to comfort others.

"Can I pray about it, Mary Ann?" she asked. They hung up the phone. Jeanie prayed several times over the next two days. She sensed God's peace and purpose in the open door. She called Mary Ann back and agreed to do it. Because of her poor health, she brought her friend Mary Jane Behan to assist her; the two of them stayed at Jim and Mary Ann's home. Jeanie enjoyed spending time face to face with the couple who had encouraged her via telephone so often over the past eight months. The Misiuks had a large, close family like the Bracas and a strong love for God that made Jeanie feel like she had known them for years.

Jeanie, Mary Jane, and Mary Ann pulled up in front of Calvary Chapel Lake Forest in Orange County, CA. The stately Saddleback Mountains rose in the background under an azure sky. God had brought her here to share a special message, and she sensed His presence with her.

When Jeanie stood up to speak in front of the ladies on that beautiful afternoon in May, she prayed for God to give her His words. After praying, she spoke honestly about her life—accepting Christ during Christina's illness, serving God with Al, losing him in 9/11, clinging to the promise that he was in heaven, trusting in God as her husband, and wanting to live for God's glory. She shared portions of Psalm 46.

God is our refuge and strength, a very present help in trouble.
Therefore we will not fear, even though the earth be removed,
And though the mountains be carried into the midst of the sea;
...There is a river whose streams shall make glad the city of God,
The holy place of the tabernacle of the Most High.

God is in the midst of her, she shall not be moved;
God shall help her, just at the break of dawn.
The LORD of hosts is with us; the God of Jacob is our refuge.
Psalm 46:1-2, 4-5, 7

Speaking of her close relationship with Christ, Jeanie said, "He's taught me a lot. He's loved me a lot, and He's been my best friend."

She spoke about Al being a witness for Christ at work, and that she believed God had a special reason for having Al there that day. For 16 years, Al had prayed for his coworkers and shared the Gospel with them. "We know—because people sent emails and someone was able to get through and leave a message by phone—that Al had about 50 people in a circle and was praying them into the kingdom. I believe with all my heart that, on that day, those men were finally listening to him," she said.

She added, "Am I saddened that God decided to take my husband home that day with those men? Yes, I am saddened. But God is my rock, my fortress, and my deliverer." Many eyes filled with tears. After she had finished speaking, Jeanie spent almost half an hour counseling and praying with several ladies in the front of the sanctuary.

After the last woman left, Mary Ann showed Jeanie to the ladies' room. Finally alone, Jeanie suddenly broke down crying. Mary Ann gave her a hug. Through her tears, Jeanie said, "I didn't know this was going to be so emotional—so hard, to relive it and to talk about it." Holding each other as sisters, Jeanie and Mary Ann prayed for God's peace. After a few minutes they dried their eyes.

"Jeanie, that was so powerful. I know God will use it," Mary Ann said.

"Praise God," Jeanie said, her voice raspy from weeping. "I just want Him to get the glory."

The next day, she shared a shorter version of her testimony with the entire congregation, again declaring that the Lord was her strength. The group of men and women seemed encouraged and responsive.

Later, when she was talking with Jim and Mary Ann, they urged her to visit other churches to speak. She realized that God was opening doors for her. During that visit, she also shared at a ladies' Bible study at Calvary Chapel Costa Mesa, CA.

As word spread about her message, other churches invited her to come speak. With every invitation, she would first ask God if it was His will before she would travel or accept speaking engagements. Ever since her heart failure in 2000, she had only a small percentage of her heart functioning. That—and the emotional strain of speaking about the tragedy—meant that she could not go unless the Lord gave her special strength.

Often she would call Pastor Jim to pray with her for God's direction, inspiration, and discernment. She went to numerous churches, schools, and other venues to share her story. She was thankful that, despite all of the pain, God could use it for good. Her work on earth wasn't finished—and neither was the impact of Al's walk with Christ.

Meditation

The Lord GOD has given Me the tongue of the learned,
that I should know how to speak a word in season to him who is weary.
He awakens Me morning by morning, He awakens My ear
to hear as the learned. The Lord GOD has opened My ear;
and I was not rebellious, nor did I turn away. Isaiah 50:4-5

Every morning, get alone with God and open the ears of your heart to Him. Read His Word and listen to what He may be saying to you. Sometimes He will even give you a message to share with another person that day. Don't turn away from His voice; keep listening.

Chapter 24

EXALTING GOD, CHALLENGING THE CHURCH

I will bless the LORD at all times;
His praise shall continually be in my mouth.
... Oh, magnify the LORD with me,
and let us exalt His name together. Psalm 34:1, 3

Just a few months later, she was back in Southern California with several speaking engagements lined up at various large churches. Staying in the home of Mike and Sandy McIntosh, she was able to enjoy their fellowship and encouragement privately. Mike was the pastor of Horizon Christian Fellowship in San Diego, and he had invited Jeanie to share her story with his congregation.

It was a beautiful Sunday morning in July, 2002. Standing behind the podium at Horizon, Jeanie prayed silently as she looked out at the congregation of more than a thousand people. Pastor Mike had just introduced her as the widow of Al Braca, a man who had died while leading people to Christ in the World Trade Center on 9/11. Thunderous applause echoed for several minutes as Jeanie waited at the platform to speak. The applause died down, and she took a deep breath.

"Thank you very much," she said, her Staten Island accent echoing through the huge sanctuary.

She opened her Bible to Psalm 34 and read:

> *I will bless the LORD at all times;*
> *His praise shall continually be in my mouth.*
> *My soul shall make its boast in the LORD;*
> *The humble shall hear of it and be glad.*
> *Oh, magnify the LORD with me,*
> *and let us exalt His name together.*

She added, "That's what I'm here for—to exalt the Lord; to tell you what a wonderful God we serve; and how faithful, loving, and kind He is during times of trouble."

She shared the story of Christina's illness, God's promise, and the little girl's miraculous recovery. She shared how she, Al, and all of their children had come to know Christ as their personal Savior, and how God had been working in their lives over the last 25 years.

"We were all doing well, all walking with the Lord, serving God. Then about three years ago, I started having menopause problems and bleeding very heavily. ...Right now, I'm another miracle; I'm working on only 16 percent of my heart. But I want to tell you that God is totally faithful." She paused to allow more applause to die down.

"Everybody thinks that 9/11 was the beginning of my deeper walk with God, but it wasn't. The minute you give your heart to Jesus and allow Him to really take over your life, the journey begins. You have to die to yourself—put your plans on the shelf. Allow Him to rule your life; you must surrender everything. Maybe for you today, that means surrendering to God in your job. Al didn't like where he was: He called it 'Sodom and Gomorrah' because of all the wickedness that went on. But he relied on Jesus totally. He would tell me, 'Jeanie, I'd love to get out of there, but I know I can't. I am the only Bible they are ever going to hear. It's the end times. I have to tell them about Jesus before it's too late.' I didn't know how right he was."

She recalled how Al had ministered to coworkers and others in his building during the bomb incident in 1993. She had assumed, on 9/11, that Al would come home again after spending hours helping people. That night, after her children had called Jeanie's doctor to secure a prescription for her weak heart, they told her that the towers had fallen and that Al had surely died. She added, "Everybody was afraid that I would be the one to go first, but he was. ...We never think it's going to happen to us. We read about tragedies, and we think it only happens to other people. I thought I was safe, that I was doing all the right things. Al and I—our whole household—we were serving God."

She paused. "People ask me, am I angry? Am I mad at Bin Laden? No. That's not what God wants for me. He has poured out His love on me, and my job is to pour His love into others."

She urged the group to trust in God. Looking around the room, she said, "No matter what happens in your life—you might be very sick, have cancer, a bad heart; your kids might be sick; someone might tell you your child is dying—surrender it. Surrender all your problems, all your worries to the Lord Jesus. His shoulders are so much bigger than ours. He loves us."

Paraphrasing 1 Peter 5:7, she said, "Cast all your cares on Him, because He cares for you."

Jeanie said gently, "No matter what happens in your life, don't be afraid. I have gone through so many heartaches in life, but I want to tell you that God is faithful."

She played a recording of "Well Done," a song that a musician named Wayne Tate had written especially for Al:

> *"He was a man with one simple plan: to follow.*
> *He loved his God; he loved his dear wife and family.*
> *At the start of each new day, he humbled himself to pray.*
> *I can almost hear the Father gently say,*
> *'Well done; well done. You've been faithful, and I'm proud of*
> *you My son.*
> *Well done. Well done. You have run your race and now your*
> *time has come.*
> *Well done.'*
> *See it's not how much you have but it's how much you give*
> *away.*
> *It's denying everything to help someone find the way.*
> *Well done."*

She added, "'Well done'—I know that's what God said to my husband. I challenge you: Will you win the lost at any cost, for Jesus? Will you start speaking to the people God brings before you and tell them of His mercy and love?"

She reminded them that the Word says a believer must speak God's truth in a loving way, as Al had done with their future son-in-law, Greg. By allowing God to love Greg through Him, Al had been able to introduce Greg to Christ. "Above all, we must love one another. The love that Jesus poured out on us, we must pour out to others. It's great to tell people they need a Savior, but if they don't see His love in us, why would they want that? They have to see His love in us; we have to be imitators of Jesus."

She felt the Lord fill her with a fresh boldness. "We need to get serious about sharing our faith because we are living in the end times," she said. "You never know when God is going to call you home. Make sure you're doing what is right, what God has called you to do."

She read 1 Thessalonians 5:1-23, part of which says,

> *But concerning the times and the seasons, brethren, you have no need that I should write to you. For you yourselves know perfectly that the day of the Lord so comes as a thief in the night. ...*
> *But you, brethren, are not in darkness, so that this Day should overtake you as a thief. You are all sons of light and sons of the day. ...But let us who are of the day be sober, putting on the breastplate of faith and love, and as a helmet the hope of salvation. ...*
> *Now may the God of peace Himself sanctify you completely; and may your whole spirit, soul, and body be preserved blameless at the coming of our Lord Jesus Christ.*

She had come to the end of her message. "Thank you so much; God bless you," she said. Hundreds of people rose from their seats and applauded.

Pastor Mike MacIntosh led the massive crowd in a prayer for Jeanie and her family. As she went back to her seat, he challenged the congregation to listen to Jeanie's words. He shared the Gospel and gave an opportunity for those in the sanctuary to respond. Several people came forward to pray and receive Christ as their Savior.

She watched the people praying to receive the Lord. With tears in her eyes, and feeling emotionally spent from sharing, Jeanie thought, *Praise God!* She was so thankful to be a part of men and women coming to Christ; it gave her a deep joy to see Al's testimony impacting so many people. And in her heart, she felt that—in a way—she and Al were still ministering together.

Meditation

I will bless the LORD at all times;
His praise shall continually be in my mouth.
My soul shall make its boast in the LORD;
The humble shall hear of it and be glad.
Oh, magnify the LORD with me,
and let us exalt His name together.
Psalm 34:1-3

As Jeanie did, will you exalt the Lord today? Will you choose to praise Him in your heart? Not only does our praise please the Lord, but it lifts us up as we remember what He has done for us. It lightens our burdens and helps us to have a heavenly perspective.

Chapter 25

ENCOURAGEMENT
AND CONFIRMATION
IN TIME OF NEED

Oh, send out Your light and Your truth! Let them lead me.
Psalm 43:3a

Despite the joy she felt in sharing Al's legacy of faith in the fire, it seemed as if something was trying to steal her confidence. She believed it was her spiritual enemy filling her mind with doubts, but she had not talked to anyone about it.

She knew Al's character—that he was always sharing Christ, that he had prayed fervently for the salvation of his coworkers, that he was bold in proclaiming the truth—but nasty doubts had been nagging her when she was alone. Could she really prove it? Was she sure that he had been praying with people that day? She was telling thousands of people—what if she was wrong?

She went over the evidence in her mind, reasoning with herself: *I saw the emails myself and so did Pastor Ray; I talked to a lady who knew the family who got the voice message on their phone about Al; I talked to police officers at Ground Zero who had heard the same stories. It has to be true.* She didn't know who she could talk to about these doubts, but she prayed that God would give her confirmation again of the truth. "I just want to be sharing the truth, Lord. Please show me," she prayed.

Finally, sitting with Sandy MacIntosh in her living room, Jeanie voiced her fears. "Sandy, something's really been bothering me. I feel so confused. What if everything I'm saying didn't really happen?" Jeanie said. "What if I have to stand before God someday and answer for telling people lies in His name?"

The two of them had been waiting for Mike to come home with some burritos for dinner. He had been praying with people at the church after the Sunday evening service when they left. "Why don't you ask Mike when he comes home?" Sandy said.

A little while later, the three of them were sitting together, and Jeanie asked Mike the same questions. "Mike, when was the first time that you heard of Al Braca?" Jeanie asked.

Mike recounted his involvement with the 9/11 tragedy. As a member of the National Disaster Response Team, he had been assigned to fly to New York City to serve as a chaplain and oversee the other chaplains ministering at three areas: Ground Zero, the morgue at the Medical Examiner's offices, and the Family Assistance Center. Mike left immediately but was waylaid by canceled flights. He arrived on September 14. "I heard about Al the first night I was there," he recalled. While he was serving at the Family Assistance Center, he heard that one of Al's coworkers had called his wife to tell her that he loved her. The coworker had said, "Al Braca is praying with people up here on this floor."

Mike thought for a moment, then added, "I heard it more than once. One time I heard that there was 'a Christian at Cantor Fitzgerald' who had been praying with people in a circle. Sometimes I heard the name Al Braca." When he heard others testifying about Al, Mike said, "It just gave me peace. I knew it was a God thing."

Jeanie let his words sink into her heart. She knew the Lord was answering her.

He went on, "Later, when I saw your son Christopher speaking about his father at the PNC Bank Arts Center, it clicked. I realized that Al Braca was Christopher's father and your husband. I told Christopher what I had heard about his dad. That was right before I met you. Remember, you said, 'Aren't you Sandy MacIntosh's husband?' I thought that was great, because no one had ever asked me that before!" The three of them laughed, since Pastor Mike—who has traveled the world teaching and meeting with government leaders in many countries—is usually considered more well-known than his wife.

Pastor Mike and Sandy prayed for Jeanie, that God would protect her mind from fear, doubt, and other attacks of the enemy. Jeanie felt encouraged. God was so good, so kind. She realized that He had brought her all the way to California, not only to strengthen the church but also to give her the personal confirmation she needed. How good it was to hear the truth from a trusted brother in Christ who had been a head chaplain at Ground Zero and had heard of Al's witness. Again she prayed simply, *Thank You Lord! You are taking care of me!*

With a new peace, she went on to share her story at several other Horizon Christian Fellowships in Southern California; she joined several pastors' wives in encouraging the women at Calvary Chapel South Bay, CA. Recounting God's faithfulness strengthened her faith. She had never dreamed that she would stand before so many, or that the prophecy about Al's far-reaching impact would come true so quickly. She watched as the Lord used Al's legacy to encourage His church again and again. It became clearer to her that this was part of the reason that the Lord had allowed Al to be taken that day.

Meditation

If any of you lacks wisdom, let him ask of God, who gives to all liberally and without reproach, and it will be given to him. James 1:5

Is there something that has been troubling you? Is there something that has been nagging at your mind, stealing your peace or confidence or joy? Take it to the Lord; ask Him for wisdom. He will give it to you freely.

Chapter 26

TOUCHING THOUSANDS
IN NEW YORK CITY

Sing to the LORD, bless His name;
Proclaim the good news of His salvation from day to day.
Psalm 96:2

Almost two months later, Jeanie again shared the stage with Pastor Mike—this time at a large "Festival of Life" outreach in the heart of Manhattan. The week-long crusade drew thousands of people. While it had been nearly a year since the terrible tragedy, Jeanie was amazed at how God used the outreach to touch so many in the area who were still hurting. *Al would have been so happy to see this,* she thought several times as the week unfolded.

More than 1,000 believers from Horizon Christian Fellowship, other Calvary Chapels, and various other Christian churches across the U.S. traveled to New York to reach out during the crusade. They fanned out through the city's five boroughs that week, distributing bags of food in low-income areas, dressing as clowns to reach out to children, and going to the various precincts and fire departments to share God's love. As a result, thousands attended the evening meetings and heard the Gospel.

Christian police officers from all over the country shared their faith with other officers in the New York area. Believers brought gifts from their fire or police departments back home. Their acts of love opened doors to minister to hurting cops, pray with first responders, and spend hours talking and listening with police, fire, and emergency workers.

Every night for a week, starting on August 26, thousands of people packed into the Salvation Army's Centennial Memorial Temple on West 14th Street in Manhattan for free Christian concerts and a

Gospel message presented by Pastor Mike. The auditorium has seating for 1,600 people, but many nights there was standing room only as people of all ages packed the main floor and the wrap-around balcony. Then Jeanie gave her testimony, sharing how Al had died in 9/11 and was now in heaven with Jesus. She told them how he had prayed with several of his coworkers before their building collapsed. Each night, she urged those in the crowd to give their hearts to Jesus, as no one knows when their time will come.

Pastor Mike gave an invitation for people to accept Christ as Savior. Night after night, Jeanie's heart leaped to see throngs of people coming forward to follow Christ. She would stay near the front, and many would approach her after hearing her testimony. The fact that she was a fellow New Yorker and had also lost a loved one gave her a deep connection with them. One after another, women came to tell Jeanie how they, too, had lost a loved one in the attacks or were going through a deep grief. Jeanie prayed with each of them, encouraging them to trust in Jesus. She wrote their names down and committed to pray for them in the months that followed.

Many expressed amazement that Jeanie was able to talk about her loss without anger or bitterness. Some said that they knew other people who had lost loved ones and had been crippled emotionally by the incident. Jeanie expressed compassion for the hurting, and gave Jesus the glory for her peace of mind. She knew that, without Christ, she could not stand firm in His love as she was doing. She was grateful that God was using her life to encourage others and to give Him glory.

After the Festival of Life crusade was over, a Christian reporter named Dan Wooding asked Jeanie her impression. She replied, "I have been so excited to see so many people come to the Lord. Lives have been changed!" Asked what advice she would share for those who were still hurting, she said, "Those who are saved need to have a deeper relationship with Christ. Those who are not saved need to know Christ as their personal Savior. I know that God has led me here to encourage others. I am going to continue as long as the door is open to me."

Exhausted but euphoric, Jeanie praised God with her family that He was still doing a mighty work in the wake of such a devastating tragedy. She again remembered the prophecy from the Caribbean pastor's wife—that Al would impact countless lives around the world for Christ. Again, God had fulfilled that promise. It wasn't the way she would have chosen, but she knew Al would rejoice to see how God was using his faithful life and faith-filled death for His heavenly kingdom.

Meditation

"Draw near to God, and He will draw near to you."
James 4:8a

Continue to draw near to the Lord today—seek His presence, ask Him to make Himself real in your life. He will answer: He will draw near to you.

Chapter 27

A STRANGER
BECOMES A SISTER

For I am not ashamed of the gospel of Christ,
or it is the power of God to salvation for everyone who believes.
Romans 1:16a

Not only did Jeanie share at large churches and massive outreaches, but she continued to minister to people one-on-one as God opened doors.

One day soon after the Festival of Life outreach, Jeanie was driving home from doing her grocery shopping. She spotted a young woman on a bench outside St. Mary's Church, a few blocks from her home in Middletown, NJ. She was sitting alone in front of a statue of Mary in the church's little garden.

As Jeanie drove past, she felt the Holy Spirit urging her to talk to the young woman. She turned the car around and parked outside the church. Getting out, she approached the young woman with a smile.

"Hello," Jeanie said. "I know you're going to think this is crazy, but I saw you—and I was going to keep driving, but the Lord told me to come talk and pray with you."

The woman didn't seem surprised, only sad. Trying to control her emotions, she related, "I'm afraid that I'm going to lose my child. I'm at my wit's end; I don't know what to do. I came here to pray, but I didn't know if God would hear my prayer."

Jeanie didn't know exactly what the woman meant, but she could tell that she was hurting. "God did hear your prayer—this is obviously an appointed time, Him bringing us together like this," Jeanie said. "He loves you. He loves you so much that He sent His only Son, Jesus Christ, to die for you."

Jeanie related the plan of salvation to the woman: That all have sinned, but Jesus died for the sins of the world, so that whoever believes in Him can have eternal life instead of eternal punishment in hell. She repeated:

For all have sinned and fall short of the glory of God. Romans 3:23

For the wages of sin is death, but the gift of God is eternal life in Christ Jesus our Lord. Romans 6:23

"God wants you to believe in Him, to accept Him as your personal Savior," Jeanie said.

She added, "I lost my husband Al in the World Trade Center a year ago. I know that he is in heaven with Jesus because he gave his life to the Lord. I know that I'm going to see him again someday because I've accepted Jesus too." The young woman looked at Jeanie with interest; she was listening.

"God wants us to trust Him—to surrender ourselves to Him: all of our problems, our past failures, our sins, our fears, our children, our entire lives to Him," Jeanie said. "He will forgive our sins. He will take our burdens and be our Comforter." Jeanie briefly related that God had been her Comforter for the past year.

The woman was still listening attentively, as if she was absorbing what she had just heard. Jeanie asked, "Do you want to accept Jesus Christ?"

With emotion, the woman said, "Yes. Yes, I do."

Jeanie led her in a prayer to God, asking for forgiveness for her sins, thanking Him for sending Jesus to die for her, and inviting Him to come into her heart.

After they prayed, Jeanie said, "Now you need to get in the Word. You need to read the Bible—do you have one?"

The woman said she did not. "You need to get one right away and start reading it. That's how we grow, how we hear God speaking to us, how we know right from wrong. You need to read your Bible every day," she said.

Jeanie waited a moment and then realized that she had said all that she was supposed to say to this young woman. "God bless you, honey," she said. "I'll be praying for you." She gave her a hug, then got back in her car and drove home.

That night she did pray for the young woman. She realized that she didn't even know her name. "Thank You Lord, for letting me show another soul into Your kingdom," she said, feeling humbled and grateful that God was using her. Before 9/11, she would not have had the courage to share Christ with a stranger; now, the Lord was using her not only to share the Gospel but to lead strangers to Christ. *It was just the kind of thing Al would have told us over dinner,* she thought, smiling as she drifted off to sleep.

Meditation

For I am not ashamed of the gospel of Christ,
for it is the power of God to salvation for everyone who believes,
for the Jew first and also for the Greek.
Romans 1:16

What a powerful message—the Gospel. With it, we can show someone the way to eternal life; we can bring a soul out of the lifetime bondage of sin into new freedom in Christ. Ask the Lord for opportunities to share the Good News with someone this week. Be on the lookout for that person. Because of your loss, you know more than some people do how near eternity can be.

Chapter 28

STONES OF REMEMBRANCE

*Each of you is to take up a stone on his shoulder ... to serve as a sign
among you ... when your children ask you, 'What do these stones mean?'
... These stones are to be a memorial to the people of Israel forever.*
Joshua 4:5b-7, NIV

Although Jeanie and her children avoided a lot of the media stories
and public events relating to 9/11—mostly because it was too painful
for them and because they chose to grieve privately—there were a few
things that had been a great comfort to her.

On September 11, 2003, a small memorial garden in their community
was dedicated to 37 of the local victims of the World Trade Center. It
was called the Middletown World Trade Center Memorial Gardens.
One afternoon that fall, Jeanie walked over to see it. On a grassy spot
under the trees not far from the train station, a path led past several
headstone-like markers, one for each victim. Jeanie stopped to look
at the one for Al. His portrait was carved on the left side of the grey
granite stone. That old half-smile played on his lips, even in the stone
carving, which had been made from a photograph.

The family had submitted the wording for the stone, and it read:

> *Alfred J. Braca—A beloved husband, father, grandfather,
> son, nephew, and friend. He made the most of life with
> all its blessings and trials. Most of all let it be known how
> much he loved his Lord and Savior, Jesus Christ.*

Yes, he did. She looked around at the grounds and the train station and
sighed. Even this train station held precious memories.

She and Christopher used to come here to meet him when he came
home from work. They would scan the crowd for his white hair, and
then Christopher would shout, "There he is! There's Daddy!" Al was

always delighted to see them, and they would talk and laugh all the way home. Then he finally got a Jeep—his first "toy," she used to call it—and would drive himself to the station. That Jeep had stayed in the parking lot for days after 9/11. She didn't remember who had finally moved it and brought it to the house.

Later, after they found his body, his Jeep keys had helped identify that it was Al. That information had been so precious in confirming that he had not jumped to his death in panic but had passed calmly into the arms of his Lord. Later, she sent the items which had been on his person to a 9/11 memorial museum called Tribute WTC Visitor Center in Lower Manhattan. The coins and keys were encrusted with a white gritty substance—probably the white ash that had covered everything—and the credit cards had been torn nearly in half from the force of the collapse.

She was glad that she had chosen to never see his remains. She didn't want to remember him that way. She wanted to remember him as he always was—with a smile at the corner of his mouth, his dark eyes twinkling, and his full head of white hair.

That's how he looked in the photo that ran with all of the articles. Stories about Al had been printed in magazines, newspapers, online tribute sites, and on television. Jeanie had saved many of them. He had always been known in the community; now he was known to the world. Jeanie decided to write something in her own words, a letter for Al, which she sent in to the newspaper, the *Staten Island Advance*.

Published on Thursday, January 16, 2003, her letter read:

> *Dearest Al,*
>
> *It's been a year since 9/11, the day that changed our lives forever. We miss you more than words can say. Your legacy has touched the lives of others.*
>
> *Your love and faith in Jesus Christ has reached so many lost people, that many have come to Christ because of your death.*

*Thank you for being a loving husband and father. We love
you more and more each day. We are so proud of being your
family!!*

*Love,
Your wife Jean*

*Editor's Note: Alfred Braca, 54, of Middletown, N.J., a
Sunnyside native, was a bond trader for Cantor Fitzgerald.
The father of four was a deeply committed Christian
who was part of the Evangelical non-denominational
Christian movement. He served as a deacon at Calvary
Chapel Four Winds in Red Bank, N.J. He earned the nick-
name "The Rev" from his co-workers who depended on him
to get them through the 1993 World Trade Center bombing.
He is remembered in this letter written by his wife, Jean.*

She clipped it from the paper the next day. She didn't know why, but it
was something she just needed to do.

Later, close to the two-year anniversary of 9/11, a Christian book was
published called *As the Towers Fell* by Lisa Chilson-Rose. In it was an
entire chapter devoted to Al. Speaking of spending his last moments
comforting and praying with his co-workers, the author wrote:

> *As usual, he thought of others more than himself. He stepped
> into eternity, ready to meet his Lord face to face, bringing
> with him some of those he had prayed about for so long. ...
> According to friends and family, Al Braca was a man who
> never wavered in his faith. ...never falsifying the Gospel
> by pretending that everything was okay when it wasn't.
> He knew that being a Christian didn't protect you from
> hard times. It meant that you had the faith and strength to
> get through those hard times.*

> *... All of his children said about their father: "Our dad
> didn't yell at us a lot. He taught us right from wrong. He
> trusted us, and that made us not want to do the bad things*

*that other kids seemed to be doing. He respected us and en-
couraged us all to have our own personal relationship with
Christ and find our own calling in life." They were taught
that they couldn't be saved through their parents, but had
to make that decision on their own. Eventually, all of Al's
children became Christians. ... God has been the Great
Comforter for this whole family.*[1]

It was true. God had been their Comforter. And Jeanie was proud of
reports about Al and his faith. There was so much sad publicity about
9/11, so much about death and sorrow, that she was happy that the
world heard this side as well—that God was the answer, and that
those who know Him can have peace, even in the face of death.

In 2002, there had been an article about him in the Fellowship of
Christian Athletes' magazine, *Sharing the Victory*; and one in a magazine published by the ministry, Focus on the Family. Christopher, 17,
told the reporter: "The last thing my dad did involved the two things
most important to him—God and his family. ...He loved to lead
people to Christ. That takes away a lot of the hurt and the pain."

Yes, it does, Jeanie thought when she read it. *But not all of it.* Still, she
was thankful for the articles, testimonies, and stories—small stones
of remembrance that she kept, reminders of Al and how he lived for
Christ. They reminded her to live for the Lord, too, one day at a time.

[1] Excerpted from "As the Towers Fell" by Lisa Chilson-Rose, August, 2003;
New Hope Publishers.

Meditation

Each of you is to take up a stone on his shoulder ... to serve as a sign among you ... when your children ask you, 'What do these stones mean?' ... These stones are to be a memorial to the people of Israel forever.
Joshua 4:5b-7, NIV

Sometimes it's helpful to have a physical, tangible "stone of remembrance"—something that reminds us of a time when He touched us in a personal way. It may also help to build or write a memorial to your lost loved one, like Jeanie's letter—something tangible to remember them. It may comfort or help you to make a stone of remembrance.

Chapter 29

LEANING ON HER
HEAVENLY HUSBAND

For your Maker is your husband, the LORD of hosts is His name;
and your Redeemer is the Holy One of Israel;
He is called the God of the whole earth.
Isaiah 54:5

One day early in 2004, Jeanie was alone reading her Bible. She was looking for more verses about widowhood. Her eyes widened when she came across a passage in Isaiah 54:

> *"Do not fear, for you will not be ashamed;*
> *neither be disgraced, for you will not be put to shame;*
> *for you will forget the shame of your youth, and will not*
> *remember the reproach of your widowhood anymore.*
> *For your Maker is your husband, the LORD of hosts*
> *is His name; and your Redeemer is the Holy One*
> *of Israel; He is called the God of the whole earth.*
> *For the LORD has called you like a woman forsaken*
> *and grieved in spirit, like a youthful wife*
> *when you were refused," says your God.*
> *"For a mere moment I have forsaken you,*
> *but with great mercies I will gather you.*
> *With a little wrath I hid My face from you for a moment;*
> *but with everlasting kindness I will have mercy on you,"*
> *says the LORD, your Redeemer.*
> Isaiah 54:4-8

She felt the Holy Spirit's gentle urging that this passage was for her, and God was speaking directly to the deepest needs in her heart.

She meditated on the words "your Maker is your Husband." This was what God had been showing her ever since Al was taken: that just as He was her Heavenly Father, so also He was her Heavenly Husband.

As Jeanie considered the last few months of her spiritual life—how she had drawn closer to the Lord, surrendered to Him, and sought to follow hard after Him—she realized that she was falling in love with Him. She realized that she had a depth and closeness with Christ that she might never have experienced if Al was still alive.

Her attitude of surrender and openness to the Lord was constant. Sometimes she couldn't go to sleep right away or she would wake up in the middle of the night. She would ask, "Lord, who do You want me to pray for?" Then she would spend the time interceding for her family, friends, and other victims of 9/11. If no one came to mind for prayer, she would turn on her lamp and read her Bible.

She also kept a basket next to her bed with her Bible, her notebook, Christian reading, and Bible study tapes. It was her way of keeping herself from going under spiritually; it was her lifeline. She had learned not to simply lay in bed feeling sorry for herself or dwelling on her loss.

If her mind started to drift to thoughts of loneliness or depression, she would sense His Spirit gently urging her to draw near to Him. And she would obey. She didn't have to pretend with the Lord, but she did have to choose to draw near to Him. She had never pretended or hid her feelings from Al; so she would be just as open with her Heavenly Husband.

She had learned that, no matter what she was feeling—anger, sorrow, joy, confusion—to come to the Lord and lay bare her heart before Him. She followed the admonition in Psalm 62:8: *"Trust in Him at all times, you people; pour out your heart before Him; God is a refuge for us. Selah."* She held nothing back from Christ. And He became her constant refuge—her source of peace and strength.

She had always gone to Al for advice about decisions or opportunities. Now, every time she was afforded an opportunity to speak or share her story, she would ask the Lord if He wanted her to do it. She knew that she needed to take care of her health and keep her family as a priority, so she didn't instantly jump at every opportunity. After she prayed, if she felt His approval and peace, then she would accept the invitation.

She realized also that the more she spoke to others about Christ, the more real He became to her. While she went from place to place sharing about God in front of large crowds, her times alone with Him were more intimate than ever. Her relationship was constantly growing. When she felt God urging her to trust Him or to believe His promises in a certain situation, she surrendered herself to His will. Time and again, issues arose about her health, her family, her grieving, financial matters, and other things she was not prepared for. As she brought them before God, He directed her step by step with gentle leadings by the Holy Spirit or answers in the Word of God.

In very practical ways, He also demonstrated that He was taking care of her as a husband would. Her physical health was a constant issue. Her weak heart made her susceptible to many illnesses, and there was always the risk of another heart failure. One of her greatest fears was getting sick again and not having Al to take care of her as he did several years ago.

She remembered back to the year 2000. From February to June, the Bracas were constantly going to the hospital because Jeanie's issue of blood had gotten worse. She would have to stay in the bathroom, unable to stop or control the heavy bleeding. She told Al she was bleeding, but she didn't tell him how much. She got weaker and weaker but didn't know what do.

Finally, Al came in the bathroom one day in June of 2000 and saw how much blood she was losing. "Is this what you've been dealing with?" he asked with gentleness and concern. She admitted that it had been going on for some time. He immediately went to the phone and told the doctor, "It's really bad. We have to do something for her now." The doctor decided that Jeanie needed a total hysterectomy. Despite her recent heart attack, they decided that her heart was stable enough for the procedure and that her loss of blood was getting too dangerous not to operate.

While Jeanie was recovering in the hospital, Al told her, "Jeanie, I told Pastor that I'm taking a break from the couples' ministry—from any ministry—for a while so that I can take care of you and our family."

When Al brought her home, he went right to work taking care of her—cooking meals, helping her dress, doing the laundry, keeping her spirits up by reading the Bible and praying with her. Their daughter Christina also returned early from Calvary Chapel Bible College to help care for Jeanie. It took a while for Jeanie's body to recover, but Al never lagged in his happy diligence, and he never complained. He even did most of the packing for their last move. Jeanie was almost fully recovered when they moved into their smaller home in Leonardo to prepare for retirement.

Without Al, Jeanie didn't know how she would function if she got sick again. But she would learn that, even in the face of her worst fear coming true, God would take care of her and be a husband to her in sickness as well. He would never leave her side; He would bring her through. Her part was to continue trusting in Him, no matter what He chose to do in her life.

Meditation

For your Maker is your husband, the LORD of hosts is His name; and your Redeemer is the Holy One of Israel; He is called the God of the whole earth.
Isaiah 54:5

When we lose a loved one, we can feel desperately alone. Each of us longs for an intimate connection with someone; we long for that spouse, that soulmate. The good news is that God calls us His bride; our Maker is also our Husband. Reach out to Him in that way; ask Him to be your constant companion and closest friend. He will meet you there; He calls you His beloved bride.

Chapter 30:

HEART FAILURE IN NAPLES

The LORD will strengthen him on his bed of illness;
You will sustain him on his sickbed.
Psalm 41:3

Jeanie smiled as she unpacked her suitcase. *Thank You Lord for how You encouraged those precious men and women,* she prayed silently. She had been a guest speaker at a large Baptist conference in Tennessee, where she shared her and Al's story with worship pastors and their wives. As she shared the song "Well Done" with them, both men and women had wept openly. She had sensed that the Holy Spirit was doing a mighty work among His people.

After she cleared out her suitcase, she began filling it again for her next journey—a trip to Florida to see Peggy and Gary Cuozzo. They were still like family to her. And their condo in Naples had been a source of refreshment and rest many times. Right after the attacks, she and Christopher found refuge there from the grimness and sorrow of New York City. That had been in February of 2002; this time she was going alone in mid-February of 2004.

Peggy and Gary greeted her at the airport, and they immediately fell into their usual close camaraderie. Jeanie shared about her most recent speaking engagement in Tennessee.

Soon after her arrival, one night Jeanie woke to a familiar, piercing pain in her chest. Fear accompanied the realization that her heart, which had given her so much trouble in the past, was not well. She lay still, breathing steadily, waiting for the pain to stop. Finally, at about 2 o'clock in the morning, she knew she had to get help. Stumbling down the hall, she rapped on the Cuozzos' bedroom door. Gary opened to find Jeanie clutching her chest.

"Gary," she said, her voice tight with pain, "It's my heart. I need you guys to pray for me." Both Gary and Peggy laid hands on Jeanie and began to pray. A few minutes into the prayer she interrupted them.

"I've got to go the hospital. I have to go *now*," she wheezed.

Gary quickly and carefully guided her down to the car and took off. As he drove, he realized he wasn't sure where the closest hospital was. Voicing amazement that he had remembered his cell phone, he called 911. Gary described his location, and the operator said to turn immediately. "What, right now?" he asked, unfamiliar with his surroundings.

"Yes, turn left now," the operator said. One block later, they pulled up to an Emergency Room. As hospital workers helped Jeanie out of the car, she collapsed. She learned later that doctors had to rush to her side with defibrillator paddles to get her heart beating again. Just a few minutes later may have been too late to save her.

After they took her into surgery, Gary phoned Jeanie's son David. The next day, he, Greg, and Christopher were on a plane to Naples. They walked into Jeanie's room in ICU; she hadn't yet fully regained consciousness. They were told by the medical staff that there was no way to know if Jeanie would be herself when she woke up; her heart failure and the lack of oxygen may have caused brain damage. The three young men waited by her bed. Finally, her eyelids fluttered open.

"Hi mom," they each said. She blinked at them. "Do you know who we are?" She looked from one to the other, saying each name in a raspy voice.

She murmured a private family joke. At first they looked at her, bewildered. Then she chuckled, "I'm just kidding!" Relieved, they laughed and squeezed her hands. Over the next day or so, Jeanie talked openly about the Lord—to her sons, to the medical staff, and to Peggy and Gary. Several times, Peggy and Jeanie shared their faith with the nurses. Gary led visitors in prayer at her bedside several times. But her body did not recover as quickly as her sense of humor.

Several days after her attack, Jeanie lay in her hospital room, disheartened by the continued presence of the breathing machine and the beeping heart monitor. She had been told that there was nothing more the doctors could do for her. She didn't know that doctors had suggested that her sons have Jeanie sign power of attorney over to them so that they could have her breathing machine turned off. But she could tell from everyone's faces that her condition was not good. Was she going to die here?

The medicine made her groggy, and she tried to suppress her rising panic as one of the doctors entered the room. Gary had been on the phone with his friend—a widely respected clinical cardiologist—and carefully set the phone down on Jeanie's bed without hanging up so that his friend could hear the attending physician's report.

The hospital doctor told Jeanie that she would have to be on oxygen the rest of her life, which probably wouldn't be very long. He informed her of the small percentage of her heart that was still functioning and concluded that she should go home and enjoy what little time she had left to live. Jeanie's countenance fell. Her son David turned pale and had to be put on bed rest in the hospital due to anxiety over possibly losing her.

After the doctor left the room, Gary retrieved the phone and said to his friend on the other line, "Did you hear that?" His friend, Dr. Jim Cox, asked to talk to Jeanie. Saddened and discouraged, Jeanie listened carefully.

"That man has the worst bedside manner I've ever heard," said Dr. Cox. "Now listen to me, Jeanie. There's no reason that you have to be on oxygen the rest of your life. As you rest, your heart will improve. I'm coming to see you myself." Jeanie thanked him and weakly motioned for Gary to take the phone.

A few days later, Dr. Cox was at the foot of Jeanie's bed, reading her charts and vital signs. His presence and his words were like sunshine breaking through a dark sky.

"Jeanie, your heart is going to improve. With your medical history, it's normal for your heart to be functioning at this small percentage. You'll be fine," he assured her. Jeanie had urged Peggy and Gary to stay in the room with her, and they listened carefully to the doctor's words. Dr. Cox had the nurses remove some of the machines, which he explained were no longer needed. He also ordered everyone in the room—including the medical staff—to pray for Jeanie.

After Jeanie was released, she returned to the condo lugging a small oxygen tank behind her. She sat down, lowered her head, and tears began to roll down her cheeks. "Jeanie, what's the matter?" Peggy asked.

"I'm going to be on this oxygen for the rest of my life," Jeanie sobbed.

Peggy was shocked. "Jeanie, don't you remember what Jimmy Cox said?" Jeanie shook her head no. Peggy knelt down and looked into her eyes. She recounted earnestly, "He said that you are going to be fine! You're not going to have to stay on that oxygen very long at all. Your heart will improve, and you'll feel normal again."

Jeanie looked at Peggy, blinking as she tried to comprehend what her friend was saying. She couldn't remember anything from the hospital except the first doctor saying that she would probably die soon. Peggy's words comforted her, and she later thanked the Lord that He had her friends there in the room so that they could encourage her later.

The Cuozzos held a weekly Bible study in their home. That week, Jeanie joined the group, propping up her oxygen tank and opening her Bible. Later, David said to her, "Mom, it's really amazing that you're not just laying in bed feeling bad about this. You're still studying the Bible."

"David, I'm going to be fine," she said, smiling. "God has a plan. He's not done with me yet." Nearly a week after being released from the hospital, she was flying home. It wasn't long before doctors allowed her to lay aside the oxygen tank.

Still needing plenty of rest, every evening Jeanie sat in bed reading her Bible—a practice that would sustain her for the next decade and beyond. When she was too ill to get out of bed, she would reach for the Word and seek comfort from the Lord. She would not allow herself to lie awake wallowing in unhealthy thoughts—even if she was in pain. Her weakened condition made her susceptible to illness, and she was often in bed with a cold or a severe flu. She learned that, if she were going to win the spiritual battle that accompanied her circumstances, she had to keep her mind on Christ.

For though we walk in the flesh, we do not war according to the flesh.
For the weapons of our warfare are not carnal but mighty in God
for pulling down strongholds, casting down arguments
and every high thing that exalts itself against the knowledge of God,
bringing every thought into captivity to the obedience of Christ.
2 Corinthians 10:3-5, NKJV

Whenever a thought would come to her that contradicted God's Word, she would purposefully dismiss it from her mind and pray. On her sickbed, she talked to the Lord as if she could see Him sitting next to her. She wrote in the journal the things that He spoke to her heart through the Bible or during her times in prayer.

Psalm 41:3 became very real to her: *The LORD will strengthen him on his bed of illness; You will sustain him on his sickbed.*

It was during her recovery after Naples that she surrendered to the idea of a book about Al. She called Pastor Brian and agreed to write down her thoughts. She was later featured in a story in *Calvary Chapel Magazine*. Through a series of events, the book began to take shape.

Over the next few years, Jeanie would have numerous seasons of illness. She learned to stay close to the Lord through every season by staying in His Word. Countless times she told others, "He is the One who gets me through. I wouldn't make it without Him." And she meant it.

Meditation

The LORD will strengthen him on his bed of illness;
You will sustain him on his sickbed.
Psalm 41:3

In those times when you are ill or sad or alone, God will be with you and strengthen you. As no one else can, He understands what you are going through. He is the healer of your body, mind, heart, and soul.

Chapter 31

TO HEAL THE BROKENHEARTED

"The Spirit of the LORD is upon Me, because He has anointed Me
...to heal the brokenhearted...to set at liberty those who are oppressed."
Luke 4:18

In late 2006, Jeanie was invited back to California to speak at a special Widows' Retreat at Calvary Chapel Costa Mesa. Some of her friends happily called it an honor to be invited to speak at Costa Mesa, where the Lord had started the Calvary Chapel movement. She knew it was; she could hardly believe it. But, as she had learned to do with each of these invitations, she prayed, "Father, do you want me to go? Will You keep me well enough to do this?"

The thought of encouraging other sisters who had lost their husbands struck a deep chord in Jeanie. For her, that was the real honor, and she was humbled—but she needed to be sure it was what the Lord wanted her to do. As she prayed about it for several days, she sensed His peace—a gentle affirmation that it was all right for her to go. She was grateful that He was her Heavenly Husband, that she could talk to Him about every detail of her life, and that He responded.

She sensed the Lord had a special purpose for the widow's retreat, and she settled down in her chair with her Bible to pray and wait on Him.

"Give me Your words, Father," she asked. She waited before Him, stilling her mind, focusing on His presence. She prayed for the widows who would come to the retreat—the older women, the younger women, those who were still going through their deep pain. She knew that the pain never goes away: it varies in intensity through different seasons, but it never stops. But she also knew that the Holy Spirit was the Comforter who could heal their hearts.

She opened her Bible and read for a while. When she came to Psalm 147, the words began to come alive before her. She began to take notes.

Praise the Lord!
For it is good to sing praises to our God;
For it is pleasant, and praise is beautiful.
The Lord builds up Jerusalem;
He gathers together the outcasts of Israel.
He heals the brokenhearted
And binds up their wounds.
Psalm 147:1-3

Clearly, the psalm was about praise. Praise means loving and thanking God through songs or prayers, but what about in hard times? She began to think about her life since 9/11—the cataclysmic shift in her life, all future plans with her beloved husband taken away, the heartbreaking adjustment for her entire family without their beloved Al. After the past seven years, she had learned that praise was still possible, and it was a choice. She could choose to dwell on her sorrow, her pain, negative feelings—like jealousy, fear, anger. They were always waiting for her, popping up unexpectedly in odd places. She would be out somewhere and see an elderly couple holding hands, and a deep, burning jealousy would seize her heart. All of these feelings she brought to the Lord honestly, asking Him to heal her, to change her heart to be pleasing to Him. She chose again and again to praise the Lord—every day purposefully turning her mind toward Him in prayer and reading His Word. It was the only way of getting through the pain to healing.

She began to consider things she was thankful for, reasons to praise God. She wrote down, "Praise God for His divine Word, His divine guidance, His divine care, His divine love, and the hope He gives—that He'll always provide for us."

She stopped a moment and dwelt on the word "hope." Another scripture came to mind: *"For I know the plans I have for you," declares the LORD, "plans to prosper you and not to harm you, plans to give you hope and a future. (Jeremiah 29:11, NIV)*

She remembered feeling that her life was over when she saw Al's building collapse. She couldn't even contemplate the future without him—let alone look forward to it. It seemed like she had entered a long, dark tunnel—that all the light had gone out of her life and would never return.

But over the past few years, God had shown her that He still had a plan for her life. He still had a "hope and a future" for her—for all of His children. It wasn't the future she had imagined or planned, but He had shown her clearly that her life was not over—that there were still things for her to do, to learn, to enjoy. She thanked Him for her family, her church, her friends who were walking with her through the heartache, and for the opportunities to encourage others. She chose to accept this future that the Lord had given her.

She pondered verse 3, that He heals the broken-hearted. She wanted to understand the verse more, so she got out her Amplified Bible.

"He heals the brokenhearted and binds up their wounds [curing their pains and their sorrows]." Psalm 147:3 (AMP). She sensed that God wanted to bind up her wounds, the wounds of the widows who would attend, and all of His children who are broken-hearted. He was the only one who could. She would talk to the ladies about how other things could never heal the deep wounds inside—no possessions, no people, no money, no indulgences, no plastic surgery, none of the things that people do to feel happy. The pain was too deep for that; the only one who could reach that far was the Father.

She made more notes. To experience that healing, one had to have a personal, intimate relationship with God. The only way to know Him was through faith in His son, Jesus Christ. She thought: *Without being born again and having the Holy Spirit in your heart, you can't hear from God. You don't know him.* She wrote: "We need to know beyond a shadow of a doubt that we are saved, sanctified, and sealed by the Holy Spirit."

Having the Holy Spirit in one's heart was required for true hope. As Romans 5:5 said, *"Now hope does not disappoint, because the love of God has been poured out in our hearts by the Holy Spirit who was given to us."* The Holy Spirit is the believer's connection to God's love. When she was lonely or sad or discouraged, the Holy Spirit would whisper to her heart without audible words that God loved her and was with her. She felt His presence every day.

Jeanie meditated more on the psalm. Part of knowing God is worshipping Him. Despite sorrow and disappointment, believers must worship the Lord—acknowledging Him, thanking Him, loving Him. The amazing thing was that worship has an effect on the worshipper. She remembered times of sweet worship with the Lord; it was as if losing herself in adoration and praise had been bandages on her broken heart. She had felt His peace and comfort—even joy—after praising Him.

It was amazing how God always knew what she needed, where she was at mentally and spiritually. Through the past seven years, she had felt so many emotions: fear, numbness, anger, confusion, sadness, grief, depression. She had also struggled with thoughts: keeping her mind on the truth, on positive things, instead of what she did not have. God understood each phase of the journey—more than she did. She wrote down: "No matter how we're feeling right now as widows, God will meet us exactly where we are. He is going to do all the work for us. But we need to have faith to believe. And we have to step out in faith and allow Him to work in our lives." There was a time to weep and grieve, but there was also a time to rise up and step out in faith. He still had a plan for those women, and for her.

She remembered Jeremiah 31:3, which says:

The LORD has appeared of old to me, saying:
"Yes, I have loved you with an everlasting love;
Therefore with lovingkindness I have drawn you."

She realized that she had been drawn to God—not by something good inside of her, but by His gentle loving kindness. He had sent her sisters to tell her about Jesus. On that dark day when she was weeping over her daughter and opened the Bible, He had miraculously made the page open to that wonderful promise that Christina would be healed. He had pursued her. He was still pursuing her, drawing her to Himself more and more through the years. She wrote down, "God is the one who draws us closer to Him. We are to submit, to surrender, to love God—and He'll do the rest."

She thought about God's divine guidance in her life. After 9/11, she had been lost, confused, hurting. When she finally received an insurance settlement, she—like many other survivors—had tried to fill the void with shopping.

But God had gently shown her that buying gifts for other people, for her children and grandchildren, could not satisfy the deep pain in her heart or in theirs. He gently guided her back toward Himself as the only true Healer. She would tell the ladies to check their hearts—to ask God to show them if they were trying to fill that emptiness with anything of the world, any material possessions, drugs, alcohol, other relationships. It was hard to imagine being happy again when you were grieving. That's what all the shopping had been about—trying to feel happy again, to make others happy, to fight off the sadness. "This is how we can be happy again—through God's guidance," she wrote.

It was important to keep growing, to keep walking with God. Being part of a Bible-teaching church was essential. She needed to hear God's word taught in truth, to have other believers to pray for and encourage her. She needed to pray for them and encourage them. God had used Christian books, praise music, fellowship, and His Word to guide her through the valley of the shadow of death, as it said in Psalm 23. He helped her through her grief, through big decisions, through times when she needed wisdom for herself or her children.

"God will give you the guidance if you're willing to meet with Him—and you've got to. Every day and every night, you need to sit at His throne and say, 'Lord, I cannot do this without You.' If you don't do this, you'll fall," she wrote. "Your spirit will close up, your heart will get hardened, and God will no longer be able to use you."

She knew it was a continual process. One had to sit at His feet, to read the Word, to be honest with God, to pour out the anger and confusion and fear and questions—and then let Him comfort and answer through His word. "Don't be ashamed to cry, or to cry out to God. He understands," she wrote. She realized that God had known even before He took Al that Jeanie would be all right—that He would be with her, equip her to stand fast and not give up, and strengthen Her through His word.

It dawned on her that if someone had told her before 9/11 that she would lose her Al but God would use her to encourage other grieving widows—she would not have believed them, she would not have been able to fathom having that kind of courage. She thanked God that this was part of His amazing plan for her. Despite her bad heart and her illnesses, He had kept her here to be His messenger.

She put aside her notes and her Bible and thanked God for speaking to her heart, for letting her see so many things that He had been doing over the past few years. She truly was able to praise Him. She asked God to minister to the widows through her—to give her His message, His words, to comfort the brokenhearted and bind up their wounds.

Meditation

He heals the brokenhearted and binds up their wounds
[curing their pains and their sorrows].
Psalm 147:3 (AMP).

If you are brokenhearted, God wants to bind up your wounds, the deep-down wounds in your heart. He cares about you and about your sorrow. Let Him in; trust Him with your grief. Don't hide it or be ashamed. He is the healer of your soul.

Now hope does not disappoint, because the love of God has been poured out
in our hearts by the Holy Spirit who was given to us.
Romans 5:5

Sometimes, after a devastating loss, hope seems impossible—almost ridiculous. But God has put the Holy Spirit in your heart to heal and comfort you, and to give you hope even after sorrow.

Chapter 32

MINISTERING TO WIDOWS

Wait on the LORD; Be of good courage,
And He shall strengthen your heart.
Psalm 27:14a

In January of 2007, Jeanie stood before a small crowd of ladies at Calvary Chapel Costa Mesa. Women of all ages were seated at round tables. Almost all of them were widows.

She shared the message from Psalm 147 that God had given her. Some had tears in their eyes. She could see the pain, the hunger for truth, for something to hold on to. She knew some were so recently widowed—their husbands having died in combat overseas—that they hadn't gone through their deepest mourning yet. She wanted to be real with them—completely transparent. She wanted to comfort them with the comfort she had received from the Lord. She wanted to give them Jesus—the only One who could meet their deepest needs.

She shared about her life with Al—the blessed, mountain-top times—when God had done amazing things for them and through them, together.

"Al and I had Bible studies in our home. We had to clear out the furniture to make room for all the people filling the house. People were getting saved and baptized in our pool. Our kitchen table was where men and women came and cried their hearts out—asking us to help them with their marriages."

Al had ministered to each one with such care, such compassion. Later, after he had been taken, Jeanie felt confusion. Why would God take a man who had been serving Him so faithfully?

"I remember asking the Lord, 'Didn't we do it all right, God? Didn't we do what Your word said?'" She paused. They were quiet, listening intently. She knew those painful questions were like gasoline on the fire of grief. "What do you do, when you think you have this perfect life? We were excited about the word of God; we used our home for God. What do you do when something this horrible happens? And all you believed in—doesn't God say He'll protect us? Why didn't He make Al stay home that morning?"

She remembered asking God that question. Jeanie looked out at their faces. Somehow she sensed that many had these same painful questions in their own hearts. There was an invisible bond in the room; they were all connected in the deepest of ways—through their faith in Christ, the loss of their beloved, and their desire to find healing. In a way, just being together that day in that safe place was a comfort.

She told them about how Al had been a witness on Wall Street, how some colleagues had mocked him, put pornography on his computer, tried to embarrass him. But he had prayed for them. And she believed with all of her heart that—at the end, when they all realized their time was up—he had been there, praying with them, and that his death had not been in vain.

Looking back, she could see God's kindness. She told them about the night before he died—that they had shared things they never had before, reminiscing about their marriage, acknowledging all the things they had learned from each other. It had been a gift from the Lord. She hoped it would remind the ladies of the special times with their husbands—those precious moments of love and intimacy, memories that they could cherish, that no one could ever take away from them. She hoped they would see that those were gifts from God.

Another special gift, just before 9/11, was their wonderful, romantic trip to the Bahamas—just the two of them. They had created beautiful memories that were now so precious to her. She mentioned the prophecy that the gospel would be shared around the world through Al. God had been fulfilling that since 9/11.

"That prophecy has certainly come true, without a shadow of a doubt," she said. "I've talked to so many people—to Dr. Dobson, to Oprah's magazine. A film crew from Japan followed me around for months—they were so impressed with our ladies' Bible study. Pastor Adrian Rogers invited me to speak. I was on TV. God has been using Al's legacy and his testimony all over the world."

She told them about her heart failure in Naples, and about the depression she went through because of her heart problems. One day she was so deeply discouraged that she felt like giving up; she asked the Lord, "Am I going to die?"

She had sat waiting for some kind of answer, her eyes blurry with tears. She was at a friend's house, and sitting in front of her was a daily bread calendar with scriptures. The verse displayed was:

Wait on the LORD;
Be of good courage,
And He shall strengthen your heart;
Wait, I say, on the LORD! Psalm 27:14

She recounted how, in that moment, in her darkest hour, He had answered her again. "Can you believe that—that He would strengthen my heart? My *heart*." She knew beyond a doubt that the verse was for her, a promise from God that He would strengthen her—not just physically but emotionally. Now, as she had grown a little stronger bit by bit, she was serving in the women's ministry at her church when her health allowed.

"I'm so happy that I get to fellowship with those women, that I'm in the word, that God has taken my life and given me a future and a hope!" Her heart was brimming with emotion—she was crying now, and beaming.

"I've seen a lot of miracles, ladies," she said. "I can truly say with Paul, 'that the things which happened to me have actually turned out for the furtherance of the gospel,' in Philippians 1:12. Praise my God! I hope that someday we can all meet again. Thank you." As the room filled with applause, she looked around at the dozens of teary-eyed, smiling faces. Afterward, several ladies approached her to pray, share their pain, or thank her for the encouragement. She knew that God had done a work in all of their hearts that day.

Meditation

Wait on the LORD; Be of good courage,
And He shall strengthen your heart.
Psalm 27:14a

In what ways are you waiting on the Lord in this season? Is your heart troubled or afraid? Keep your eyes on Jesus, trust in His goodness and His plan. He will strengthen your heart.

Chapter 33

FAITH:
A CONTINUAL CHOICE

*You will keep him in perfect peace, whose mind is stayed on You,
because he trusts in You.*
Isaiah 26:3

Later in 2007, Jeanie received a phone call from a writer at *Calvary Chapel Magazine*. She was lying in bed due to illness, but she was happy to share about what God had been doing in her life. They prayed, then talked about 9/11 and Jeanie's continued faith in God over the years.

The young woman asked her if trusting God was a conscious, deliberate act of the will.

"It is a choice," Jeanie said. "I do believe it is a choice. I think that if you know what the Word of God says, you can stand on God's promises because of who He is. He says He'll never leave us or forsake us."

Asked about grief and sorrow, Jeanie replied, "When you're in that state of mind, or if you get as sick as I did, you've just got to keep close—close to the Word of God. Fill your mind with Scriptures, even when you're the sickest and the lowest."

Jeanie looked around her; laid out beside her on her bed were her journal, Bible, and teaching tapes. "Like right now, I have my Bible open and I have been listening to a church tape. Even though I'm too sick to go, I try to stay plugged in."

They talked about her recent trip to Calvary Chapel Costa Mesa, CA, and ministering to widows. "It's a privilege to know who Christ is, and not to question things any more. So I went to California, and now I'm in bed for three weeks. I'm content where He has me. I can be victorious, even in bed right now."

She paused. She didn't want to sound despondent; she wasn't. In a way, she was thankful for the times that she had to stay in bed. "You get to know Him in a deeper way. But you have to make choices every single day. When I can't breathe and can barely lift my head from the pillow, at least I can put a tape in, lay my head back down, and listen to the Word of God. Those are the times you need to stay closest to Him rather than filling your life with other things that aren't really important. And you are the one who has to make those choices."

They talked about her intimate relationship with Jesus Christ. "It really is my life—Christ is my life. He's the breath that I breathe. He's everything. He lives in us. We're one in Christ. We're in Christ; there's no separation there—we don't have Him in some things and leave Him out of others. But it's our choice to continue on and on with Him until He calls us home or the rapture comes—whichever comes first. We must abide every day."

They talked about the challenges that come with grief and illness. Jeanie spoke candidly, as was her custom. "The enemy can come in very quickly—especially if you're weak physically or emotionally," Jeanie said. They discussed patterns of grieving in her life and others.

"I can see it in women all around me. If they're not saved, there's a bitterness that unfortunately comes on. And they may think that materialistic things—like having the money we received from the government—will make you feel better. But it's only like a band aid—nothing that will last, even with the superficial highs you might get. There have been women on talk shows who got plastic surgery or traveled here and there, but I know they are still sad and empty. I've talked to them. The reason I still have a wonderful peace and joy is because my hope is in Jesus Christ and not in material things."

Some of the 9/11 widows and children felt that the money was "blood money," and struggled with guilt or anger. She had found freedom and balance in the Lord. She and her family had used some of the money for a much-needed vacation, viewing it as a blessing from the Lord. Everyone needs to evaluate what is truly helpful to them and practice those things. They stuck together as a family, preferring to spend time together on the anniversary of Al's death rather than going to 9/11 memorial services to be reminded of the horrible things that happened. They often talk about their father together and cherish his memory.

When asked why her testimony had encouraged so many women, Jeanie said, "I can't speak for all Christian women. Their being at the retreat to hear my testimony was an encouragement to me. I think it took a lot for those women to be there—many of them are mothers, daughters, young widows with children, and older women."

She remembered talking one-on-one with ladies at the retreat. "I think we need to be honest with one another. I think we should be able to cry when we need to cry and be open about our emotions and feelings," she said. "But we also shouldn't use that as our crutch. Instead, it's a way to let the Holy Spirit cleanse us, renew us, and allow us to work through that pain. We need to go to the Word of God and praise God even when life is hard."

She added, "Many times I didn't have the strength to go to church physically or even to praise Him out loud, but I could practice that in my mind and stay in close contact with God. We can't allow the world to come in with its lies."

Jeanie's personal testimony of how the Lord was using her life was featured in the Fall 2007 issue of the *Calvary Chapel Magazine*, which was distributed worldwide to more than 40,000 readers.

As Jeanie looked over the article, which included a picture of herself and Al smiling together at Deanna's wedding, she praised God that He was still using her life for His glory. *It is a choice,* she thought. *Lord, I want to keep choosing You. I want to hear you say, 'Well done.'*

Meditation

Finally, brethren, whatever things are true, whatever things are noble, whatever things are just, whatever things are pure, whatever things are lovely, whatever things are of good report, if there is any virtue and if there is anything praiseworthy—meditate on these things. Phil. 4:8

Where are your thoughts? It is important for you to choose healthy and truthful thoughts. When we think of what is true, that is what is true according to God's perspective, not mere earthly circumstances. Ask God to give you His perspective on your life, to give you His thoughts.

Chapter 34:

STAYING THE COURSE

Do not remember the former things,
Nor consider the things of old.
Behold, I will do a new thing,
Now it shall spring forth;
Shall you not know it?
I will even make a road in the wilderness
And rivers in the desert.
Isaiah 43:18-19

In the years following the widows' retreat, Jeanie continued to walk with the Lord—going through various seasons. There were difficult times of illness, but there were also wonderful times of ministering to the ladies at her church and enjoying her family.

Something within her was changing. She was discovering a new identity—beyond widowhood. She explained to a friend, "Life goes on, and people need to go on and not focus on 9/11. I don't want to be known any more as the widow of 9/11."

Her life was about so much more than that. "[Losing Al] was a journey that God took me on. It was part of my life, but it was many years ago. I have so much more to offer, to tell others. I want to share Jesus with them."

God was using her to encourage ladies at her fellowship about their day-to-day struggles. "Sometimes they just need someone to listen to them, or some advice, or a shoulder to cry on. For some people, it helps them to see that, 'If Jeanie could get through this, then I can too.'"

She kept a daily dialogue with the Lord through her prayer journal.

New Year's Day 2009 was a joyful contrast to New Year's 2002—the first without Al. She opened her journal and wrote:

January 1

Dearest Lord,
Today starts a New Year, Jan 1, 2009.
May Your will be done in my life and the life of my family.
Complete what you have started, allow us to grow in the grace
and knowledge of our Lord Jesus Christ.
Keep us close to You. Guide us and keep us safe. Protect us and help us
to glorify Your name. We are Your children; You are our Abba!
Lord, we were born to please You. Help us to do so.

Col 1:10. "Walk worthy of the Lord, fully pleasing Him, being fruitful in
every good work and increasing in the knowledge of God."

Love, me
XOXO

Two days later, she had an infection in her lungs and was confined to bed. It was hard to breathe, but she pulled out her Bible and journal.

January 3

Thank You for being a Savior and Healer to me. Once again I'm recovering
from a lung problem. Thank you for bringing my [friend] into my life as a
blessing.

As the quiet hours stretched on, she reflected on her life. Was she doing what God wanted her to do? Later that same day, she wrote,

Dear Lord, what pleases You about my life?
Do I obey You, worship You, please You, love You, praise You?
Please show me! I do want to. You're a God that deserves the best of me.
Love, me

In the midst of her illness, Jeanie and her family had big choices to make about their home. Because of her poor health and need for care, they had consolidated homes. She was living in a downstairs apartment while some of her children and grandchildren lived upstairs.

She prayed daily, seeking the Lord for guidance. She had learned well that He was their Father now; they needed His wisdom to make decisions.

January 9
Lord Jesus,
Preside over every aspect of my life.
May I see Your glory as You direct my path.
I love you Jesus with all my heart.
Please give me wisdom as I seek Your face.
"Though He slay me, yet will I trust Him." Job 13:15a
...You are faithful, O God. You are near to me, guiding me
with Your loving care.

January 13
We have decided on the house; we have peace.
Thank You Father! Praise You! You are "a father of the fatherless,
a defender of widows"(Psalm 68:5). You will take good care of us!
... I will not be afraid but remember all the good that You,
my God have done in my life. Always sustaining me, healing me,
guiding me, and loving me. Showing me Your great love and mercy...

Psalm 37:5:
"Commit your way to the LORD,
Trust also in Him,
And He shall bring it to pass.
You have spoken to me through Psalm 37.
I will meditate on these promises..."

January 19
Dearest Savior,
I love you!
These afflictions that I have been given, may they always honor
and glorify you. May my eyes always be on You and not how I feel,
or how I can't breathe, but on who You are Jesus.

There is nothing impossible for those who diligently seek the Lord.
My hope is in You only.
May your will be done.
Amen

Jeanie's illness continued for weeks. Over the next few years, she would have trouble with her heart, as well as periodic colds and flus, which her weakened immune system was susceptible to. Despite all of this, she contined to keep her eyes on the Lord until her death in October 2014.

A LETTER FROM JEANIE

September 2014

Dear Reader,

The best gift I could ever give to you and the world is my Jesus.

I want to introduce Him to you, as the very real friend He is to me. As you read these pages, I hope you hear, "This is Jesus—here, take Him, learn of Him, and love Him. And get to know Him like I did."

Because of 9/11 and my illnesses since then, I have learned to trust in Him. My trust is from moment to moment because of the depth of my heart condition. I don't plan vacations. I ask the Lord, "Is it OK to go on a vacation? May I go? Will you keep me healthy?" Then I have a group of people pray for me that He keeps me healthy. I died in Savannah, Georgia, for seven minutes. But He let me come back.

Thirteen years have passed since 9/11. There have been many days of heart failures, operations, a severe hysterectomy, weeks and months in bed.

Sicknesses have overcome me, but my faith in Jesus is still strong. Trusting in Him in all things has become a little easier each time. Some days I have to lie in my room recovering from asthma attacks and other illnesses. Some days I can get up and serve with my church or at outreaches. The one who sustains me is my Lord. Sometimes it's for weeks or months that I must stay in bed.

Even alone in my room, these are the days of restoration—of drawing closer to my Savior and my Lord. I read His Word, I listen to worship music. I send cards and encouragement to people.

More grandchildren have come, and life goes on. Friends have come, friends have gone. But Jesus is still with me, loving me and caring for me just as He has promised. He has kept His promise to take care of me as my Husband, now that Al's gone.

Thirteen years later, my white chair is no longer white; it is striped and blue. I still sit at my desk a lot, studying God's word.

I still have days of tears, but my joy and my peace come from my relationship with the God of all creation.

How great is that?

Thank You Lord, for always being a wonderful, faithful God.
My prayer, Lord, is that I could leave a legacy for my wonderful children and grandchildren, as my husband Al has.

I love You,
Your daughter Jeanie

To Bethany, Gabby, and Hannah,

Your Pop Pop loved you very much. The days he spent with you brought him much love, joy, and happiness that he had never known or could ever have dreamt of.

To Alexandra, Matthew, Caleb, Joshua, Luke, and Nicholas,

Pop Pop would have been so proud of you all, and his prayer would be that you would always follow Jesus all the days of your life. Even though he never met you, his love is ever present and is always with you.

The best gift I could ever give my children and grandchildren is Jesus. My prayer is that you would learn from Him as he teaches you to forgive, and always allow others to feel loved, just as Christ has loved us.

Pray. Pray, my children.
Always stay close to Jesus and study His Word.

Love,
Nana

CPSIA information can be obtained
at www.ICGtesting.com
Printed in the USA
FFOW03n2245250317
33703FF